Allerton Bywater

Allerton Bywater
Copyright © 2007 Bruce Haywood
All rights reserved

ISBN 978-1-880977-21-7

First edition, first printing—March 2007

XOXOX Press
102 Gaskin Avenue, Box 51
Gambier, OH 43022

website **http://xoxoxpress.com**
email **books@xoxoxpress.com**

Printed by Printing Arts Press, Mt. Vernon, Ohio
Book design by Jerry Kelly
Printed in USA

Library of Congress Cataloging-in-Publication Data

Haywood, Bruce.
  Allerton Bywater : memories of a Yorkshire boyhood / Bruce
Haywood. -- 1st ed.
       p. cm.
   ISBN 978-1-880977-21-7
  1. Haywood, Bruce--Childhood and youth. 2. Allerton Bywater
(England)--Biography. 3. West Yorkshire (England)--Biography. I.
Title.
   DA690.A3754H39 2007
   378.0092--dc22
   [B]
                                                2007004979

Allerton Bywater
Memories of a Yorkshire Boyhood

Bruce Haywood

XOXOX
PRESS

For my daughter Margaret,
who knows the truth of this.

Allerton Bywater

Members of the Allerton "Ladies Bright Hour" in costume for a concert, most certainly a fund raiser. Their annual event was a highlight of the Methodist year. My mother never took part.

Chapter 1
My Village

Allerton Bywater: my village's name comes trippingly from the tongue, inviting the hearer to imagine the bucolic English village of travel posters. The name is unmistakably English, at home among such Yorkshire neighbors as Appleton Roebuck, Church Fenton, Market Weighton.

The "water" that flows by my native place quickly destroys any notion that Allerton—our everyday name for it—is a lovely place, despite the village's full name. The truth is that it is as ugly a place as you will find in all England. My youngest aunt liked to claim that, in a contest in the nineteen-thirties to identify England's least attractive village, Allerton Bywater had won first place. For a long time I believed her story was true. The River Aire, which rises at a Yorkshire beauty spot some thirty miles northwest of my village, passes though Leeds and Bradford before it reaches Allerton. In the years between the two world wars, the years of my childhood, those industrial centers ruthlessly poured their wastes into a once pristine stream, polluting, killing fish, and giving the river a repellent odor. Two miles downstream from Allerton, where the Aire pours over a weir at Castleford, detergents were whipped into a foam that then floated over near-by streets; blobs of it would fall onto the light tan raincoats of those waiting for buses, marking them permanently. Happily, efforts to clean up the Aire in recent years have freed Castleford from that menace.

Yet in my childhood the fields along the river between Allerton and Castleford were the most inviting place to take a walk and in good weather we often saved bus fare by walking the two miles to the town. It was there, too, that I walked with "my" dog, Peter, who was in truth my grandpa's Airedale terrier, the surrogate for the dog my father would never let me have. Peter spent most of his days on a chain in a tiny back-yard and he was grateful when I, a little boy still, took him for walks through those fields along the river. I was allowed to do so occasionally, after being warned by the one grandparent or the other not to let Peter get into the river. They had obviously never taken him for a walk beside the Aire, for that always rambunctious dog, who would fetch thrown sticks untiringly for hours, could never be fooled into retrieving a stick from the river. I can see him now, charging along after the flying stick that was just beyond his jaws, only to come to a screeching halt, as he detected the river's stink and slammed on all four brakes. Reluctantly, after years of trying, I gave up on Peter and rejoiced in my unearned reputation as a "good boy" who heeded his grandparents' admonitions.

Small though it is, Allerton Bywater can properly claim to be a village, because it has a church, which is to say an Anglican church, the premises of the official and established Church of England. Were there no church, it would be called a hamlet; the English are not careless with nomenclature. A town, bigger than a village for starters, is an incorporated community with a mayor and town council, but, no matter how large it may grow, it cannot be called a city unless it has a cathedral. Such distinctions speak to the history of a country where church and state have not been constitutionally separated and where nice distinctions are prized.

Though the river's waters gave my village its name, the Aire did not give it its identity. That came from the coal mine that was Allerton's reason for existence. The pit, as it was usually called, employed nearly all the men and older boys of the place. It was the last mine on the eastern edge of the Great Yorkshire Coalfield that westward fathered scores of mines and provided the fuel for millions of fireplaces. Looking west from my village, one saw all the horrors of the industrial revolution, in one grim town and village after another, while eastward was rural England, mostly unspoiled, looking much as it must have looked for those many centuries that the land had been settled.

My mother's father went to work in the Allerton mine when he was only eleven, my father when he was thirteen. My paternal grandfather and his six sons all found employment there; for some of them it was a life-long job. So did men from nearby communities, who rode the buses in their work clothes, their faces and hands black with coal dust, seated menacingly beside housewives on their way to shop. To my village had come men from Ireland, Scotland and Wales, as well as from other counties in England, seeking work and wages they could not find at home. The "newcomers" were forever viewed as outsiders, though their children were as Yorkshire as we were, indistinguishable in their appearance and their accent from the children of the long-established folk.

The pit was omnipresent in Allerton life. Coal dust floated everywhere in the air, to be washed into the earth eventually by heavy rains. My mother, house-proud, often dusted twice a day on the worst days and for most women window washing was a weekly chore. In the days before electric dryers, laundry had to be hung outside on a line, where it was sadly vulnerable on bad days to the falling coal dust. I can remember my mother's lip-curled sigh when she brought in a basket of clothes that had been spoiled. Whenever I went back for a visit in later years I could immediately feel the coal dust between my teeth, its presence quickly on my scalp. We never escaped it.

The miners worked eight-hour shifts, three shifts every day except Sunday, and I would see them walking wearily home, still in their "muck," as we called it, coal-soaked clothes and flat caps, their faces like so many black-face comedians of minstrel shows, eyeballs startlingly white, dentures gleaming. And every day I would see men whose bodies had been ruined in the pit: some legless, some with an arm gone, some whose broken backs condemned them to permanent confinement in a wheelchair. Worst were those blinded by flying stone when an explosive charge, fired to open a coal seam, somehow went off prematurely. When I was pressed into service as chapel organist as a fifteen-year old, it was because our organist had been crushed by falling rock. He was a shot-firer, among the mine's elite.

The pit was an always dangerous place, the men who worked in it ever alert to its grim, threatening powers. Our society has come to accept the ruined bodies as a concomitant to having coal in its fireplaces and power plants, with not nearly enough done to improve safety. I am astonished—and not a little proud—that those Allerton pit men were cheerful and optimistic. Even those with shattered bodies most often grinned at life, gathering with their fellows in good weather on one of the several benches about the village to gossip and smoke their pipes. It was one of my childhood pleasures to hide behind shrubbery where I could listen to the men talk, even though my mother had expressly forbidden that, she fearing that I would pick up bad language. But they were not profane, respecting those among them who were chapel- or church-goers. Some of my classmates in the village school would eventually take their places on those benches, silently reminding me of the fate I had escaped.

The most visible thing in Allerton was the "pit-head gear," a pair of giant wheels atop a tall A-shaped tower, that was strongly cross-braced, its feet set firmly in concrete. One could see it from every corner of the village. Over the wheels ran thick cables that lowered cages into the mine's depths, cages that sometimes carried men, more often small, coal-filled wooden wagons that had run first along underground tramways, to go then to unloading points above ground. The wagons—called "tubs" by the miners—were pulled along those subterranean tracks by little ponies, whose lives, except for one glorious week a year, were spent in nearly total darkness. But for that one week, when the pit was closed for the annual vacation afforded the miners, the ponies were brought up to have a vacation in the open air, grazing in the fields beside the river. The day of their release was a red-letter day for the village children. We knew well in advance when it was going to be and we gathered along the street where the ponies would be ridden from the mine's entrance to the gate at the first field. The rising excitement must have matched that at Ernest Hemingway's bull runs, as the ponies came galloping towards us, ridden bareback by lads who waved their caps at us exuberantly as they flew by and gave their ponies friendly slaps on the flank with them. I have never in my life known anything more exciting. Later in the week, my friends and I would walk the fields to see the ponies, their heads down, cropping the grass. I often wondered whether it was true, as sentimental poets often claimed, that the poor creatures were totally blind.

The one week in the year when men and ponies were released from bondage was the only happy aspect to the mine. It was a place of back-breaking labor for coolie wages, a place from which for most there was no escape in a life of drudgery. My maternal grandfather left the pit when his new bride taught him to read and write (a condition she laid down in accepting his proposal of marriage), and he spent the rest of his working days selling insurance in area villages, making weekly rounds to pick up the pennies the insured paid for enough coverage to guarantee them a decent burial. He made his seven grandchildren promise never to go down the pit. I took the pledge eagerly and literally. I never broke it for even a tourist's visit, for the shattered bodies I saw every day and the talk I heard from the old gaffers made me terrified of the mine. That fear helped make me the good student that I became.

In recent years friends of mine have confirmed my sense that, for all the ugliness and drudgery of the miners' world, their morale was high; they were proud of what they were and of their ability to cope with the job's dangers and disasters. But the nationalization of the coal industry in the years after World War II destroyed their morale; they lived at an unhappy distance from the new bosses, the bureaucrats in far-away London, whose actions were often bewildering. The camaraderie of the old days was lost. I was visiting the village at a time when an ad in the "Yorkshire Post" set the miners to laughing at the absurdities they found in their new world. The ad sought candidates for the position of regional director of the Coal Board, as the government agency was called. After setting out the attributes a candidate would be expected to bring to the position, the ad concluded with the statement, "Some knowledge of coal mining would be helpful."

Being other than a miner in a mining culture could make a man feel uncomfortably alien. This was brought home to me pointedly on my first visit back to Allerton after eight years away. On my way to visit my old school in Castleford one afternoon, I rode the bus through the village, looking for familiar faces among the people who boarded at the couple of stops before we got to the pit gate. There a dozen or so miners got on the bus and, anonymously black-faced, dropped onto empty seats besides wary passengers who shifted towards the windows, seeking to protect their clothing. A slightly built young man settled in beside me, making me very conscious of the near-white raincoat I was wearing. The bus lurched off and after a minute the miner, who had been looking at me out of his eye corner, said in the dialect, "You are Bruce Haywood, aren't you?" I acknowledged in standard English that I was and he went on to say, "You don't recognize me, but I was in school with you." He spoke his name and I immediately recalled the lad who had sat a couple of aisles over in classrooms from me for five years. I remembered that he had left school at sixteen, after earning the School Certificate, to become an apprentice in an accounting firm in Leeds. I was at once both startled and curious that he had become a miner, after he had had the same opportunity to escape the pit that all of us at that school had enjoyed, but before I could ask him what had made him choose the mine, he quizzed me about life in Canada and the States. My emigration, I quickly gathered from him, had made me something of a local celebrity and he was eager to learn what my new life was like. He got off at a first stop in Castleford before I had had a chance to ask him about his own life, but I found out from mutual friends what had made him give up a white-collar opportunity for pit work. He had first elected to go into the mine when he reached eighteen, taking an option open to all in our area during the war to work in the pit rather than go into the armed services. Then he had married a local girl, the daughter and sister of miners. With his wartime service done, he tried to return to the career he had made a start on, but he found himself excluded from family gossip and made to feel like a traitor to his class. So he had gone back to the pit, staying home with the dialect and familiar idiom. For him, he had told people, it was preferable to being shut out. I heard subsequently of a couple of others who had made the same choice.

But for those who decided to break away, to "emigrate" within England, so to speak, there was a tricky game to be played On that same visit I was given an example of the price a schoolmate was paying for his decision to seek to escape his origins. I was waiting at the bus stop close to my parents' home when I became aware of a little woman at my elbow, snuffling and saying something in the dialect that I recognized eventually as "You are a good lad, Bruce. You come home to see your mother." Then I recognized her as the mother of a classmate who had exploited a war-time opportunity and become a success in industry in the south of England, a fact my mother had reported to me with emphasis in a letter years earlier. But it was old school friends again who were able to tell me all the implications of my classmate's breaking out. He had "made it" financially and had married well, his wife a child of the middle class in southern England. By carefully masking his origins, he had been accepted into the middle class. He had escaped, as I had, but he did not dare risk a return to the village, lest that lead to somebody's discovering his masquerade. He sent money occasionally to his parents so that they could take the train down to visit him and his family, though he concealed them in his home during their stay. England's class system does not allow easy movement from one level to another and those who manage to move up a stage live in fear of being called fraud.

The pit was emphatically a man's world. For the girls of the community the mine offered few opportunities: a handful of jobs clerking in the offices or serving in the canteen. Most of them finished their formal schooling at fourteen, as did the boys, and their job opportunities were essentially two: either they could work in the clothing factories for which Leeds, nine miles away, was famous, or they could go "into service." Simply put, the choice was between running a sewing machine or being a maid. Before World War II every middle class household in England had at least one maid, often a resident cook as well, and there seemed always to be a demand for nannies, too. So my village sent many a girl off to work in the stately homes of the aristocracy or in the less-than-stately homes of the middle class. The consequence was sometimes, alas, a sixteen-year-old girl returning to the village, impregnated by the master of the house or his adolescent son, to bear an illegitimate child (the term was cruelly applied in those days), and to suffer the tut-tuts of the village's elders. One of my mother's sisters bore such a child and lived thereafter in my grandpa's home, her son raised as though he were her brother. My cousin Jack, seven years older than I, was my "uncle" until I was fifteen, when my piano teacher unwittingly broke the truth to me, something my mother had never been able to bring herself to do. I was too shocked then to ask my mother about it and the deception continued until Jack had children who called my aunt grandma. Many years later, when I was in my sixties and Jack dead the year or two, my mother finally spoke of the sad history and apologized for having misled me. She had, of course, been simply a part of a well-intentioned family conspiracy. Even then it was very painful for my mother to admit Jack's origins. Her father, she said, had been disgraced and she still grieved for him. Of her sister nothing was said and I was left to imagine the hell she must have lived in.

There was no way to keep such a secret in my village if a pregnancy had advanced beyond a few weeks, for Allerton was small in every respect. I knew everybody in the village, most of the dogs and cats as well. I believe there were fewer than two thousand of us and we knew who was "church" and who "chapel," who were the teetotalers and who went to pubs, who were the hard workers and who the drones, which men beat their wives and which helped with the housework, who owned a bicycle and who (rarely) a motorbike. There were only three cars in the village, two of them owned by our one resident physician, the third a rakish MG two-seater owned by a man who had known success in the larger world and who had come home, still unmarried, to spend his retirement in his sister's house. I dreamed of matching his success and of some day having an MG just like his, but by the time I could afford one the classic MG was no more.

Most people lived in public housing, as did we until I was eight, or in tiny brick hovels built in depressing rows by the mine owners. Pit houses and public were alike in having two stories, with two rooms up, two down. They were alike, too, in being cold and damp. The only heat came from open fireplaces, burning the coal that was always readily available, for the miners received a cart-load regularly as part of their pay and usually had enough to sell to men like my father. The houses were alike in having gaslights and no electricity, but differed in their sanitary arrangements. Whereas those of us in public housing could rejoice in having bathrooms, the poor folk in the pit rows had "middens" at the end of their little backyards. Those were toilet and trash bin alike and the village had workers who shoveled out the contents periodically through a hatch half way up the outer wall. Rats lived there in profusion and the bolder boys would pull open a hatch door to view them scampering about among the garbage and filth. My mother would never walk on the side of the street next to the middens and my fear of rats kept me over there too.

Remarkably, both my grandfathers had managed to buy larger houses on opposite sides of the street that ran from the mine entrance. While both houses had running water, neither had a bathroom or an indoor toilet, but my mother's father had had a flush toilet installed in place of the "one holer" that was original equipment. It was a mighty cold place eight yards from the back door and on rainy days that was a long sprint. Both grandfathers made the same provision in their wills, namely that after their death the house would be available to whichever children wished to live in it. On my mother's side, two unmarried uncles and the unfortunate aunt took advantage of the provision; on my father's side, his oldest sister and her married daughter occupied the house without other kin. Working class folk didn't challenge wills.

In the days before markets and malls lured shoppers from the village, there were several shops, ma-and-pa operations all. Four fish-and-chip shops were open six nights a week and a couple of lunch hours as well. There was a flourishing bakery, a couple of butchers, two small groceries, two general stores, and in what would have been the front room of their house, my maternal grandma sold boots and shoes. (That seemed to inspire my mother's sense that her family was nearly middle class, or at least that they belonged in the upper level of the working class.) The husband of my father's youngest sister was the village barber, plying his trade in the front room of his dwelling. Several women ran "salons" in their kitchens or front rooms, all of them, I imagine, operating without licenses. We were pretty self-contained, with the only compelling reason for most people to go into Castleford, a town of twenty-five thousand or so, being to go to the movies.

Allerton was obviously a place of limited horizons and enclosed lives. Except to shock, I have not found it easy to impress people with its features. Indeed, the only attention-getting line about my coal-mine world I have ever been able to come up with is that my paternal grandfather worked for a time in the same pit as the father of Henry Moore, the celebrated sculptor whose hollowed pieces have seemed to some critics an evoking of the hollowed earth he walked as a child.

And now Allerton is without its pit, a discovery I made a few years in a chance reading of "The Economist," which had an article on the village's uncertain future. The economics of a depressed industry had led to the mine's closing and I have wondered what my village can be like without it. Where do the boys, leaving school, find jobs? What now gives the place its identity? What can it be like with no coal dust in the air, with no great wheels from which to get one's bearings? I have no kinfolk there from whom I can seek answer and, like me, my childhood friends have left for greener pastures.

The Haywoods in 1912—six sons, four daughters. The survivors. My father is second from the right. At that point, all six brothers and their father were miners.

My maternal grandfather, William Street, in a rare studio portrait.

Chapter 2
The Ancient County of York

Like Caesar's Gaul, the Yorkshire of my childhood was divided into three parts, each called a "Riding." The word came originally from Anglo-Saxon "thridding," the ancestor of our modern "third." People changed "thridding" mistakenly to "the ridding" and then "the riding," probably through association with the verb "to ride." Indeed, I once heard somebody claim that the boundary of a Riding was the distance a man could cover on horseback in one day. No rider could travel in one day around one third of England's largest county by far. Yorkshire is roughly sixty miles across and approximately the same distance from its northern to its southern limit.

In truth there is no political entity called Yorkshire today. Only fond memory and staunch local patriotism keep the idea of a Yorkshire alive. Some years after World War II a Labor Party government, perhaps intent on destroying local loyalties in order to strengthen the central government in London, undertook a massive reorganization of the shires, redrawing county lines, changing names, and inevitably creating many new bureaucracies. Thus they declared the ancient county of York a thing of history and in its stead created a handful of new counties, one of them, the former West Riding more or less, to be called henceforth West Yorkshire. (That was the name of the regiment I did infantry training with in World War II before my transfer to the Intelligence Corps.)

But in my young days there were Ridings called North, East, and West. Roughly equal in size, they differed greatly in character. The North Riding, known to many television viewers through the adaptations of James Herriot's delightful tales about a Yorkshire vet, is the best part of all England, most Yorkshire folk would agree. It is a place of lovely, fertile river valleys, collectively called the Dales, where loose-stone walls gird farmers' dramatically sloping fields. Between the valleys, on the "tops," as the locals say, are bleak, wind-swept moorlands where the soil is extremely thin and where heather and gorse predominate. There sheep graze in open pasture, their sides marked with painted "brands." A motorist must be alert for their sudden rushes across the narrow roads that wind across the moors, particularly when anxious ewes have their lambs about. The villages are rustic and charming, destinations for tourists in cars and buses these days, while streams sparkle everywhere with bright water and ripple gaily over polished stones.

East Yorkshire is flat and open, a place of grazing Holsteins, modest villages, and, eventually, vacation towns along the North Sea coast. That coastline, with its rugged cliffs and screaming seabirds, is being gradually eaten away by winter storms, while on the other side of England the Irish Sea steadily adds to the beaches. Thus year by year, inch by inch, England moves slowly away from Europe, something ardently to be wished for, some Yorkshire folk would say.

Allerton is unhappily characteristic of what is to be found in the heavily industrialized West Riding. The most densely populated part of Yorkshire, its cities and towns are dull, dirty, and without charm. My native heath is obviously not sought out by tourists and visitors from other countries. It is known for the products of its industries (Sheffield steel was once world famous), for its professional rugby players, and its cricketers. And before nationalization ruined a once healthy industry, it was famous for its coal.

Yorkshire, the County of York, was the first great Viking territory in England. After decades of raiding the Yorkshire coast, the Vikings moved inland and, finding rich farmland, put down roots and added their North Germanic genes to an already mixed pool of Roman, Celtic, and West Germanic elements. Their language was sufficiently close to the Yorkshire form of Anglo-Saxon that there was easy communication between the invaders and the settled people.

The city today called York had once been a Roman citadel. The Vikings gave the place the name "Jorvik," the "vik" part of the name being the common Scandinavian word for a town on water. Not long after World War II workmen excavating footings for new buildings in the city center came on a hoard of Viking relics that has become the holdings of the finest Viking museum in the world. It alone is reason enough for tourists to seek out York (now in the County of North Yorkshire), and, indeed, the Viking Museum has become one of Britain's most visited places.

York is the unofficial capital of the northland, the counterweight to London in some degree. Two hundred miles north of England's capital city, York sits on a line of latitude that runs through the lower part of Canada's Hudson Bay, yet thanks to the Gulf Stream it enjoys a mild, even climate the year round. One of my father's proud boasts was that he always had a rose to bring in from his garden on Christmas Day. (But to grow tomatoes he had to build a greenhouse, heated on even some summer days with a little coal stove. One of my chores was to tend to that stove, a job I was always able to combine with feeding the chickens.)

York is a lovely, ancient city of deep historic interest. Venerable white stone walls surround the city's center and a walk along their top provides a fascinating view of streets so narrow that people can shake hands, leaning from upstairs windows. There are lovely stretches of flowered parkland along the River Ouse, up which the Vikings doubtless rowed their boats when first they came.

The city's greatest pride is its cathedral, called the Minster, a name which, like the "Gate" that is used instead of "Street" in the center of the city, speaks to the Viking heritage. The Minster is a national monument, seat of the Archbishop of York, who is the second ranking prelate in the Church of England. Its treasure is the largest assembly of stained glass windows in the world, all of it carefully removed and buried in the ground at the very beginning of World War II.

The memory that I carried off to America of my only visit to the cathedral was of a Minster with plain window glass. Imagine my astonishment and wonder when, visiting the Minster years later with my wife and daughters, I saw the stained glass in all its splendor. As I write, my mind recaptures the ethereal glow of those lovely windows. Glory to God in the highest!

In the last years of my mother's long life—she survived my father by ten years—I experienced a slice of Yorkshire life so different from the life I had known in Allerton that I might have been in a different country. In order to get my mother away for a time from that awful place she had spent her whole life in, I rented a cottage in rural North Yorkshire, far from the madding crowd, where she spent two weeks with my two teenaged daughters and me in simple, but altogether pleasant quarters. (By then my wife had developed a fear of flying and stayed home.) There in the Dales the air was clean and fresh, the June days so long that there were but a couple of hours of near-darkness before the birds began their morning song. It was a place of old stone houses and well-tended little yards, with a stream that flowed gently through the quiet village. It was a place from which to take drives in our rented car on twisty, narrow roads over the heather-clad moors, a place to attend the ancient parish church on Sunday mornings (with very few others), a place with a charming local pub where my daughters and I, leaving teetotal grandma to watch TV, drank a beer with the locals. On days when rain kept us in the cottage I was the chief cook and bottle-washer, while Margaret and Elizabeth kept my mother entertained. Truth demands that I report that one daughter always helped me with the dishes.

One day, after our mid-day dinner, it was Margaret's turn to keep my mother company, while Elizabeth and I washed and dried. My mother's saying that she had never really had an idea of how we lived in America, despite the yards of home movie film I had sent over the years, brought Margaret to ask, "Why didn't you ever come to visit us, grandma?" Margaret had often heard me report that, in response to my urging my parents to come, my mother always offered the same excuse: "Oh, we don't know anybody over there, but if you come to see us you'll be able to see all your relatives and friends as well. So it's better that you come here." Now, all my friends had long ago left the Allerton area and I didn't see any need to visit aunts and uncles so frequently, but I had always yielded to what I thought was simply my parents' fear of flying. Margaret pressed for a reply: "You really should have come." There was a pause and then, plainly audible to us in the kitchen, came finally the truth: "I was afraid I might die over there." My dear, deeply Yorkshire mother could think of no fate worse than having death find her away from Allerton.

In later years my daughters talked more often about those fortnights in rural Yorkshire than they did of our travels in Europe or our stays in London. Like me, they valued the brief encounters with a way of life centuries old, with the simple routines of country living, watching cows being guided along the road to pasture in the morning, seeing them come back at milking time in the evening. We lived as the North Yorkshire folk lived. Being like them without a refrigerator, I took my basket and shopped daily for our food, at the butcher's and the baker's, at the little market where shoppers still pointed at a shelf and asked a clerk to take an item down from there. I asked the locals about the weather forecast, my no-longer-Yorkshire accent getting me curious looks, and I picked up a newspaper at the same shop where I bought the English chocolates all four of us liked for dessert. Of an evening we watched the very good and the awful of English television, always amazed at the number of American programs the BBC purchased for its viewers. I was fascinated to discover that my mother, not recognizing the visual clues that would allow an American viewer to date the era of a program, thought that the Chicago of Al Capone, the early West of "Bonanza," and the Kentucky frontier of "Davy Crocket" were all the America of her present time. When I undertook to correct an impression of American mores she had wrongly gathered from some program of ours, she said that the program must be a truthful representation of life in America, else our government wouldn't have allowed it to be sold to the BBC. How many other people in England and elsewhere, I have since wondered, get their "truths" about our country from what they take to be government-sponsored television programs? I had to convince my mother, after we watched an Eliot Ness episode, that I would be perfectly safe in attending a professional meeting in Chicago.

Those stays in the Dales also allowed us to dine occasionally in lovely country hotels, more often than not on duck or North Sea fish. With no point in England being more than sixty miles from the ocean, fresh-caught fish is always a menu feature and we particularly relished plaice, a flatfish that is, I believe, found only in the North Sea and is everywhere in England considered a delicacy. But getting my mother through the doors of those hotels was always a difficult task. The simple fact was that she thought she had no right to be in such a place. She may have feared they wouldn't accept our money. Very much the captive of England's appalling class system, my mother believed that she had no right to be in what was obviously not a place frequented by the working class. The mere sight of the hotel, as we drove into the parking lot, was sufficient to get her saying, "You are surely not thinking of going in here, Bruce." Inside and seated at a white-clothed table, she was visibly uncomfortable, darting looks at other diners, conscious that her clothes were not in the price range of the things they were wearing. Dealing with a waitress was torture for her; she seemed to think that she had to apologize for taking the girl's time and attention away from better things. "If you wouldn't mind" accompanied her every inquiry or, finally, her order. Poor thing, I think she never enjoyed one bite of her food. It was at such moments that I hated the class system that had always chained my parents and had so long held me captive. Then I rejoiced in my American citizenship that had liberated me and in the fact that my daughters knew "class system" only as a curiosity that was not part of their lives.

My children loved the England of those vacations in the Dales, even as they loved London and its rich hoard of antiquities. Had Elizabeth not succumbed to cancer when she was barely an adult, I am confident that some day she would have found a way to spend chunks of every summer in Yorkshire. A short time before her death, when she knew that she had little time left, she flew to England alone, having led us to believe that she was going to New York to see her best childhood friend. She went to say goodbye to her England, just as some weeks before she had stood alone gazing out on Lake Superior, breathing a farewell to Michigan's Upper Peninsula, her mother's country, where we had spent so many happy family vacations.

My parents' wedding portrait shows my paternal grandfather on the left, maternal grandfather on the right, with one of my mother's brothers and her sisters—the smallest is twenty years her junior. Why no grandmothers? I have no idea.

Chapter 3
Detached Dad

My father, I have come to believe, had never really wished to be a father. I reached that conclusion after recognizing how indifferent he was to me and most of my activities in my childhood. He never took me anywhere, unless my mother were along. He never watched me play rugby, never came to my school's annual sports day (not even when I was the school's best javelin thrower and captain of my "house"). Though he had been an excellent swimmer in his youth, he didn't teach me to swim. He gave me no instruction in the use of his tools; indeed, I was strictly forbidden their use. He did teach me to ride a bicycle; I still remember falling off and skinning my knees. The only thing he had an interest in my becoming, apparently, was chapel organist, a position his oldest brother held for decades, so he watched my progress with the piano with evident approval. But that was it.

I was born in the tenth year of my parents' marriage, when my father was thirty-seven, my mother thirty-six. I was the first and only child. Late in her life, when my mother took to telling me things she had always kept from me before,

she confided sadly that she had desperately wanted to have a second child, preferably a daughter,
but my father said absolutely not. "There is pasture for only one calf," he said, in a phrase
unusually poetic for him, but I think four could
have lived as cheaply as three, had my father really relished the role of parent. He seemed not to
know how to relate to children. When my little
cousins or friends of mine came to the house he
was ill at ease, anxious for them to leave. He was
no better in later years with my daughters.

He was a simple man who had the minimum
amount of schooling Yorkshire expected in those
days. His last day in school was the day before he
started working in the pit. He got out of the
mine when he volunteered to serve in the Royal
Navy in World War I; there he shoveled coal to
feed a destroyer's boiler, doing a job not much at
a remove from what he had done down the pit.
My parents' wedding photograph shows him in
his sailor's uniform, already late in his twenties.
Somewhere along the way he learned how to
drive—a rare skill in England in those days—and
he decided, on being discharged in 1918, to buy
a minibus in partnership with his brother
George. They proposed to provide passenger
service to and from Castleford, counting heavily

on miners traveling to and fro, as well as shoppers and schoolchildren. But George gave free rides to folks he knew and both brothers failed to insist on passengers paying full fare, so they were soon broke and the bus was claimed by the bank. Happily for the brothers, a newly formed company in Castleford, which had won a contract for ferrying miners at the time of shift changes, took them on as drivers. That job suited my mother, for it seemed a cut above coal mining in the social scale. She would shudder when she spoke of a friend whose husband "came home with a black face." So my father settled for less pay, but a usually less dangerous life.

Bus driving was a terrible job in many ways. The hours of sitting were hard on a man's digestion. It irked my mother that my father usually had to work split shifts, which meant that he was up before dawn to drive miners to the early shift, back at home for a couple of hours in the morning, gone again to serve morning shoppers, home in the afternoon for a while, and driving again into the late evening: an eight hour day that was spread over fourteen or fifteen. Then there came the years of the blackout between 1939 and 1945, when the use of headlights was forbidden and bus drivers squinted at a road ahead of them that was barely illuminated, except on moonlit nights. On top of that were the yellow, sulphurous fogs that so often shrouded West Yorkshire roads, a mix of the smoke from thousands of household coal fires and the moisture-laden air floating in from the North Sea. Those fogs were often so bad that my father had to have his conductor walk a few feet ahead of the bus to guide him. He rarely complained, but he was drawn and weary in those years and my mother lived in constant fear that he would be killed in a wreck.

Of my parents' courtship I know virtually nothing, except that it involved occasional motor bike outings to the seaside. They grew up on opposite sides of Robinson Street, perhaps the best street in the older part of the village, but I imagine that it was at chapel teas and the like that they got to know each other. In any event, they rarely mentioned the years before their marriage and, when they did, it was to talk of others, not of themselves.

My father was able to keep his motorbike for a few years after my birth, but evidently my growing demands for food and clothing required him to give it up. I have imagined that he would rather have kept the bike and given me up, but that is on my mean days. I'm sure he loved me in his way. I was always fond of my father, withdrawn and taciturn though he was. He recognized clearly that I was my mother's child and he seemed to have every confidence that she would see to it that I was prepared for the world. Needless to say, there was never one of those father–son chats where the "facts of life" are revealed and I must say that I was glad of that. When I was fourteen or so my mother said to me, obviously embarrassed that she was raising the question, "I imagine you have found out about reproduction and such in your biology class." I hastened to assure her, blushing to my roots, that indeed I had, though the truth was that bigger boys had stripped me of my innocence long before Miss Oddy had a chance to talk about the birds and the bees. "Good," my mother said. "Of course you can always ask your father, if there's anything you want to know." Sure, mother!

My father did have his passions, quiet and withdrawn as he was. They were his garden, sacred music, and his canaries.

Our life in public housing came to an end when I was eight and my parents took out a mortgage on a newly built house, a "semi-detached villa" up on the hill at the west end of Allerton. "Semi-detached" meant that our house shared a wall with its neighbor. It was a red letter day when we moved in. We had electricity instead of gas lamps (though we had only one wall outlet), a modern bathroom, a third bedroom that became mine, a tiny space that the builder, in fact, called a box room. I eventually outgrew its six feet by four feet and had to take over my parents' bedroom, while they moved into what had before been called "the guest bedroom." How very posh!

But for my father the joy was a quarter acre of land in a narrow strip behind the house. At the far end he soon planted apple trees, beyond the wired run he created for his chickens. Then between the henhouse and our house he dug gardens for vegetables and even flowers. It was his pride that he would grow there all the potatoes, cabbages, cauliflowers, turnips, beans, peas, onions, lettuce, radishes that we could eat, so, with a dozen hens laying eggs regularly, we had something of a small farm. As I grew older I was occasionally pressed into duty for digging, weeding, or harvesting, but for the most part my father kept me off his land, even as he kept me from his tools. There could be absolutely no question of my having a dog, though I pined for one for years, for a dog would certainly dig up the garden.

The only reading my father ever did, apart from his skimming the newspaper, was in a weekly magazine called "The Smallholder," a journal of items on the successful cultivation of vegetable gardens. I cannot recall his ever quoting it or acknowledging that he had learned anything from it, but he rejected my mother's frequent suggestions that he stop buying it. I, who read everything in the house that was printed, even the labels on cans and bottles, found nothing in it to interest me. I cannot remember my father ever having a book in his hand, except the hymn book in chapel.

Good Methodist that he was, my father neither smoked nor drank. Being also a good Yorkshireman, he was usually frugal, careful with every penny. But he allowed himself one extravagance that my mother nattered him about for years. One of my earliest memories is of lying in bed on a Sunday morning listening to the trills and warbles of the canary downstairs. A German Roller, he lived in a little cage in the living kitchen of the house, where he passed his days hopping the couple of inches from one perch to the other, chirping, fluffing his feathers, bursting occasionally into his throat-swelling runs of song. And scattering seed. It was that last that brought my mother to muttering, "I could wish that that dirty bird would get out of his cage and fly out of the window." She was too Christian a woman really to wish that, but I'm sure that saying it out loud gave her some relief. The canary truly was the "dirty bird" my mother labeled him, for he scattered tiny shells in a circle beneath his cage. In the days before vacuum cleaners, keeping up with that canary was a chore my mother really resented. She could take no pleasure in his song, find no joy in his presence. I know there was as lot of tension between my parents over that constant clean-up. It was our move to the west end that brought a solution and an end to the bickering.

Not long after we were settled in, my father undertook the building of a small shed, no more than six feet square. Inside he created two flights, one above the other, and still had room for seed storage in a metal bin and space for a person to get in to feed the birds and clean out their droppings. For birds in the plural there soon were. The German Roller got something to sing about—and to. Not long after her arrival, my father installed a ceramic nest form—German Rollers seem not to know how to fend for themselves—which the female lined with feathers plucked from her breast, and perhaps his. So with time the number of canaries grew to six or seven and then, to my great joy, my father added an outdoor flight, eight feet square, a place where the colorful birds could swoop and bank about, moving from one perch to another. And there was more color to come. First it was a bullfinch, then a European goldfinch—red faced and beautifully marked—both doomed to be celibate males. Then, just a year or so before the war began, my father added a pair of budgerigars, the tiny Australian parakeets that had become all the rage in England. I was utterly fascinated by their blue, yellow, and green feathers, their gliding flights. Those Australians needed no porcelain nest form; a rough box with a hole in it sufficed. And they were prolific! My father was soon carrying little budgies to Castleford and selling them to the man he bought seed from. (Finally my mother could admit to some comfort with my father's hobby!) I spent many hours watching those birds; I brought friends to watch them with me; and they became a source of warmth between my father and me such as we had never had before. (I never fail to think of the budgerigars whenever I see that wonderful "Monty Python" skit about the Norwegian Blue.)

There were many budgies in Allerton in those days and many stories about them and their owners. People bragged about their birds' ability to say their names, for "talkers" budgies could become, if one were very, very patient. Some could count to ten, while others could recite their name and address. Inevitably a few escaped when they were allowed out of their cages and I would see a budgie ganging with a flock of sparrows, like a colorfully clad officer at the head of his khaki-clad squad. They survived England's mild winters and may have even found mates. A friend of my mother's found a stray budgie pecking at crumbs she had thrown out her kitchen door and she was able to capture it. She put the bird in an old cage she happened to have and coaxed it to speak a word. The bird remained mute, content with its surroundings and the seed she bought for it. So after a while the woman went into town and bought a modern cage for the budgie, complete with mirror, bell, and little ladder. No sooner was the bird in its new quarters than it recited its name—and its address. Bless her, the woman returned the budgie to its rightful owner.

Alas, there came a sad day for my father, the saddest he ever knew, I have sometimes thought. As we moved deeper into war, provisions of every kind became more and more scarce. My father spent many an hour traveling about seeking seed for his birds, returning empty handed more often than not. So he decided that he would end their lives rather than have them starve to death. He took a cardboard box down to the shed and put his birds in it, one after the other. Then he brought them to the house, put the box in the oven, and turned on the gas. He sat in his fireside chair and wept. I went upstairs to my room and cried, for the birds and for him. The war had come to Allerton.

My father lived twenty-four years after he retired at sixty-five, years enriched by his singing in male-voice choirs in the area and particularly by his serving as choir director for the Methodists in the village. It was a position he had long coveted, but it was not possible for him to serve so long as his bus driving required that he work two Sundays in the month. The Haywoods were musical, as my mother's family emphatically were not. Robert, my father's oldest brother, was chapel organist for three decades and he played the cello besides. Three or four of the brothers played the violin; two had fine tenor voices, while all four sisters sang alto well. My father had an excellent bass voice and sang harmony instinctively. He could read music well, but he could scarcely play a simple hymn tune on the piano. His musical tastes never advanced beyond Handel's "Messiah," the choruses from which he knew by heart, and he was happiest with the hymns of the Methodist hymn book. Those he would sing or whistle around the house or as he worked in his garden, so much so that I learned most of them simply by being around him. Though I owe to my mother most of what I cherish in my upbringing, it is to my father that I am indebted for my early training in music and the fact that I had piano lessons.

My father was only five feet six inches tall; I passed him when I was eleven or twelve. Slightly built, he was nevertheless strong and hard muscled. He showed no interest in sports, nor in much else beyond the daily round of his existence; his tastes were simple and his needs few. He did enjoy food and I have always envied him his metabolism, for he could put away mounds of potatoes and gravy, never gaining an ounce. He was obedient to my mother, never resenting the fact that when she used the word "home," she meant her father's house. When his garden and his chickens produced excess, it was to her "home" that he carried his crops, not to his kin. He never complained that I was being raised a "Street" rather than a "Haywood." His name was Joseph, usually Joe. I think his life was happy on the whole, though I fractured the dream that would have had him directing the choir while I played the organ.

My Father's long narrow garden, with chicken coops visible in the far back, and the goldfish pond in the foreground. The neighbor to the left did no gardening.

Chapter 4
Omnipresent Mother

When I think of my "English family," it is of my mother's family I think: the Streets. "Grandpa" and "Grandma" meant only my mother's parents, for I never knew my paternal grandparents, John and Anne Haywood; they were victims of the 1918 flu epidemic, seven years before I was born. Besides, my father was close to the bottom of a large family, his oldest siblings twenty-some years his senior. In consequence he had some nephews and nieces older than he was, my cousins who seemed in my childhood to be old folks. In 1986, the year my mother died, a Haywood cousin who was but nine years my senior, showed me the family Bible in which were recorded the births (and often deaths) of my father's siblings. (Somebody other than the parents made those entries, a physician perhaps, because both were illiterate.) I was astonished to see, having known so little of that history, that my paternal grandmother had, in effect, been pregnant for thirty years. She bore her first child when she was nineteen, her last when she was forty-nine. I cannot recall just how many births there were, but I remember the sad catalog of children who did not survive. And there were many, some living a day or two, some a few weeks, some longer. Six boys and four girls made it into adulthood, the large majority of them living beyond the three-score years and ten that the Bible speaks of, but which few in those hard days actually saw. Two Josephs before my father had lived only a few days; his parents obviously wanted a son with that name.

My father knew nothing of his antecedents, other than that his parents had come from East Yorkshire as newly-weds. Illiterates have no use for documents and the family Bible seems to have been the only written word the senior Haywoods valued. I have never sought to look into their past, partly because I had every reason to believe that I would find only duplicates of that sad page in the family Bible: the pain of childbirth and lost babies.

While my father was at the bottom end of his family, my mother was near the top of hers. She had a brother and sister older than she, but the flu epidemic snatched Annie away and I rarely heard mention of her. There were two younger brothers and three sisters, the last among them arriving exactly twenty years after my mother. My mother remembered several lost babies. Such families were, of course, typical in those pre-condom days. (Some sociologist must by now have written an article on the effect of the condom's becoming widely available in the nineteen-twenties and the drastic change in family size that resulted. To say nothing of the difference in the quality of life of working class women.) With two of the brothers never marrying and the one daughter remaining at home unmarried after bearing her illegitimate child, the eight Streets of my mother's generation produced only seven children. My only remaining link to my English family is the one female among my cousins: Christine, who lives in Australia and whose letters have kept me abreast of the doings of her four brothers, all but one emigrants to the antipodes.

The Streets had even better long-life genes than the Haywoods. My mother lived to be 98, the youngest of her sisters died at 80. Another made it to 99 and the other to 100. The three brothers lived into their eighties.

No member of my mother's family cherished the family more than she did. I have said earlier that 71 Robinson Street remained "home" to her throughout her life and in consequence I spent a lot of my childhood there. I did not know a Christmas Day in my parents' home until I visited them with my family more than twenty years after I had emigrated. It was the first time a Christmas tree had been in that house. My grandpa expected his children to be at his table for Christmas dinner and only Flo, mother of five and living at a distance, and Tom, married to a Jewish woman, didn't appear. I have no fond memories of Christmases in Yorkshire; it was a day when I was early dragged away from new toys, first to chapel for morning service, then— the one happy element—dinner with the traditional goose and Christmas pudding with three-penny bits in, and after that a long day of watching the adults play whist and Monopoly while I read any and every magazine and newspaper in the house. Games were interrupted for the King's radio message to his people, an occasion that always got a reaction from Uncle Bill. He was a staunch foe of the monarchy and he delighted in mocking whatever the King had to say, usually shocking my mother while amusing everybody else. Bill's favorite target in the Royal Family, however, was the husband of the King's sister, the Princess Royal, an effete aristocrat named Lord Lascelles. Bill's particular joy was to call that worthy Lord Laceholes and to denounce him for owning an obscene amount of farmland to the north of us. Of course there was a break in the game playing for tea at four, with a lot of family chit-chat, "catching up" my mother called it. The day was the more difficult for me to endure because there were no books at my grandparent's home except library books, and I was always told that they were off limits. But my mother adored the day, whether my father was there or not—and more often than not he had to work at least part of the day.

There are happier and sometimes curious things I associate with those Christmases. The holiday season was a time for friends to call and the convention was that such visitors were given a piece of Christmas cake with cheese and a glass of port wine. Even as a child I was puzzled by the fact that my strictly teetotal parents spent hard-earned money on wine and offered it to their equally teetotal Methodist friends. I never saw anybody decline a glass and I recall pleased expressions and words of praise as visitors sipped. The Christmas cake, though, was the center of attraction. It was a fruit cake, baked weeks in advance, dense with currants and raisins, and then encased in a white sugar frosting a half inch thick. That icing was so solid that a knife might be bent trying to penetrate it. My daughters used to refer to is as "concrete" and they were pleased to have been little exposed to it. Once iced, the cakes were preserved for the holidays by being carefully wrapped in tin foil and put in a tin box. Visitors were expected to comment favorably with monosyllabic expressions of praise between bites and afterwards to offer comparison with the cake they remembered from last year. French wine tasters were no more serious in their rituals. The icing, I must say, did the job it was really intended to do, for the cake was always wonderfully moist and fresh, even if some of it survived the holidays and was eaten in February. Yorkshire Christmas cake made me a life-long fan of fruit cake, to the dismay of my American friends, most of whom abhor it and often ridicule me for my claiming that it is a delicacy.

The great Christmas joy for me—and I would guess most Yorkshire children—was the pantomime. I hasten to say that "pantomime," as Yorkshire Christmas seasons understood it, had nothing to do with mime. It was the name for a sort of musical comedy, usually a well-known fairy tale like "Cinderella" or "Puss in Boots" in a version that allowed for the inclusion of popular songs, slapstick comedy, and local and contemporary references. The "panto," as it was popularly known, had its inviolable conventions. There was always a love story, with the lovers a "principal boy" (a girl, usually an alto), and a "principal girl" (a sweet soprano). There was a threat to true love in the person of "the Dame"—the cruel stepmother, the vain and malicious queen, the wicked witch—with that role always filled by a male comedian, usually a well-known radio performer. There was always a lot of interaction of Dame and audience, some of it approaching the bawdy. And always a "pantomime horse," two men flopping about without reference to the plot. Going to the pantomime meant going into the big city, Leeds, a week or two before Christmas and that was an opportunity to see the big stores in their Christmas decor. We did virtually no decorating at home; a sprig or two of evergreen poked behind a picture on the wall and Christmas cards set out on the mantlepiece was the extent of it. So seeing the gaiety of the department store windows was a great treat. It was my wish to have my young daughters know that altogether happy aspect of the Yorkshire Christmas that, as much as anything, made me propose to my parents that we come to spend Christmas with them one year. The panto lived up to my hopes and expectations; the rest of the visit was a disappointing time, with my parents puzzled by the "American" elements, like the little, ornamented Christmas tree, we injected into their Christmas and with the winter weather at its most dismal. When I asked Margaret recently what she remembered of that Christmas, her first memory was of wet slush in her boots.

Until I came along, my grandpa was the center of my mother's life. Though she loved her mother and remained devoted to her, she admired and cherished her father beyond anybody. From him came her tenaciously strong sense of family. When at twenty-seven she told her father that she wished to marry, his answer was a puzzled, "Why? Aren't you happy at home?" He was a remarkable man. An illiterate child when he came to Allerton with his older brothers, looking for a job in the pit, he learned to read and write in the first year of his marriage, becoming thereafter a hungry reader. Indeed, when I think of him, I see him silent, in his chair before the fire, his eyes fixed on a book. The book was often the Bible, which he studied exhaustively. Literacy liberated him in every way—from the drudgery of work in the mine, from the limits of his upbringing, from the little world of Allerton and its environs. Until a stroke took him at 89, he was always a healthy and vigorous man, a walker of the country lanes to the east of our village, a tireless worker for the Methodists, eventually an elected County Councillor. He had a strong, though not big, ego, knowing himself, confident in his dealings, believing himself respected. If my village had had a mayor, I am quite confident he would have been elected to the job by a very large majority and would have held it for many years.

My grandma, in contrast, was a nearly invisible figure within and without the household. I remember her either bringing dishes to the table or brushing my grandpa's collar before he left on his rounds, a folded white handkerchief on the table for him to pick up at the last minute. She died when I was a young teenager without my ever having come to know her well. My mother and her sisters obviously reacted negatively to the image of the serving, obedient, self-denying woman she offered them. They became female versions of their father: tough minded, resolute, energetic, commanding. Like my father, my uncles on my mother's side learned to play second fiddle.

Long before the word "feminist" became a part of the national vocabulary, my grandpa was one. Content to let his sons find a life in the mine, he wanted his daughters to have the opportunity to become teachers. Three of the four did. Remarkably enough, the two youngest, just two years apart in age, were sent together to a teachers training college two hundred miles away in London, which made them world travelers in Allerton eyes. Envying them that, my mother often said, though without bitterness, that she was "at the wrong end of the family," for her father could not afford that form of education for her. Hers was a tougher road to teaching.

The alternative to earning a college diploma was to work as an "uncertified" teacher, usually as a substitute for an ailing teacher, while she took night-school courses in Castleford over several years. She rode a bike over there in bitter winters; she gave her weekends to study, and she helped her burdened mother with the younger children. Once she had her certificate, she became a full-time teacher at a considerably higher salary. Not that that changed much for her, for she continued to turn over her pay package to her father, who gave her a modest allowance and took the rest for room and board. That pattern continued until she married.

My mother was a passionate teacher, finding a joy in the classroom that she knew nowhere else. She used to tell me how, when she was a tiny girl, she would set out rows of stones, pretending that those were the pupils in her classroom. Her face lit up with joy at the memory of it. So, in a time when married women were not allowed to teach, my father's proposing marriage must have brought her before a cruel decision. I am confident that, had she remained childless, she would have forever rued her decision to marry and give up teaching. But in the end the war that brought horror and suffering to so many brought liberation to my mother, for, with male teachers being drafted, the door was opened to married women and my mother taught full-time thereafter. Because her way to full-time teaching was so difficult, my mother nursed a grudge for years against Flo, who married after but one year of teaching and, as it seemed, wasted her college training. (Like my mother, Flo returned to the classroom in the war and stayed on to become a headmistress, redeeming herself in the family's eyes.) Her favorite sibling was Ella, the youngest child who, childless herself, taught for many years once the ban on married women was lifted and became headmistress of a charming school up in one of the lovely Dales.

Only one thing gave my mother more joy and satisfaction than teaching, and that was motherhood. I, the greatest joy in her life, became, alas, her greatest disappointment.

There were two phrases that rang through my childhood like a leitmotif through a Wagner opera. The one, in response to my rebellious questioning about our poverty, "Bruce, we have to know our place." The other, in explanation of behaviors or restrictions imposed on me, "I want you to be different." They provided the tensions of my childhood and my life has been a coming to terms with them.

My mother remained a captive of the class system all her life, though in her way its willing prisoner. For she was a snob, a working class snob, ever alert to niceties and distinctions. She instructed me that I was never to refer to her father as "grandad" or "grandfather" as other children did. No, it must always be "grandpa," for that seemed to her more "refined," more middle class, as any originally French form was thought to be. She spoke scornfully of the aristocracy (though not of the Royal Family), who did not "work for a living," even while she insisted on thinking of herself, the oldest daughter of William Street, as something of an aristocrat among the villagers. I often heard her claim that my father's being a bus driver put him in the "professional class," a cut above the miners who were merely "laborers." It was very important to her to make the distinction. She would say, "We are working class, there's no denying that. But we are not at the bottom." The bottom was where the miners were, together with people without skills or training. She was well aware that she had married beneath her and she did her best to try to persuade my father, who instinctively ranked himself with his brothers and the rest of the community, that he owed it to her to seek to rise above the level where he was content to float. She would not allow him to address me or her with the "thou" that in our Yorkshire speech was the familiar form of address. She fretted when she heard him use it with his brothers and sisters. Neither did she wish me to use that pronoun with my peers, though of course I did. She might rarely use it in jesting with her older brother (who habitually used "thou" in addressing her, as did her father), or she would sometimes use it as a special endearment when she cuddled me, saying

"Ah do luv thee." Equally, she tried to keep dialect forms out of our speech, an impossibility of course when they were part of our everyday idiom. Yet all her struggles did not, in the end, allow her to think that she had escaped class distinction. For one thing, she never shook off her Yorkshire accent, with its heavy consonants and pure vowels, that was always oddly paired with the standard English words she sought to have shape her vocabulary. Good manners were to her a weapon against the vulgarity of village life, as was having a table cloth at all four meals. Nose in the air, ears cocked, she fought all her life against the powers that sought to have her think of herself as no different from the rest of the village folk.

All of this had one great purpose. It was part of her plan for me, her plan that I should escape my class and go on to a life in the professional class. In fact, her dream was that I should become a Methodist minister or, failing that, a headmaster. That, she was well aware, could only happen through my becoming educated—not just schooled, but educated. She began early. By the time I was five I was reading the newspaper and she soon moved me on to books. She bought an encyclopedia—it may have been the only one in the village—and urged me to use it. Its red volumes sat in a glass-fronted cabinet close to my place at table and, through a sort of osmosis, I learned the gold letters identifying each volume so well that I can recite them today: A-BAN, BAN-CAV, CAV-DRI, DRI-GOL, GOL-JYO, K-MET, MEU-POR POR-SKO, SKR-ZYR (the last my favorite combination that I have thought of using on a vanity license plate). She badgered me to work hard in school, to set my sights on being the top of the class and, beyond that, getting a "scholarship." That word, when I was still tiny, seemed to me like an "abracadabra" that would open the treasure chest of my future, but I soon learned that it meant admission, at age eleven, to a school in Castleford and seven years of being expected to excel there. That would mean leaving the village school and most of my friends, for few children were ever advanced from Allerton; my mother knew the names of every one of them in the past twenty years or so. I did not like at all the idea of being exiled from the village five days a week.

Together with exhortations to work hard in school and to be a good boy went every-day whisperings, as she held me on her lap, that I was not going to be "like the other boys," something

I thought already guaranteed by my missing foreskin, or that she wanted me to make her proud of me. Unfortunately my imagination translated most of this into my having to do homework instead of playing soccer and cricket; the life my mother seemed to have in mind for me would mean renouncing all I held dear.

My mother loved me for myself, not just as the vehicle of her ambition for herself. She fed me well; she watched for any sign of physical weakness or illness; she showered affection on me and clothed me as well as her means would allow. Concerned always for my spiritual growth, she created a private prayer for me that I recited at her knee every evening before I went to bed:

> Gentle Jesus, meek and mild,
> Look upon a little child.
> Pity my simplicity,
> Suffer me to come to Thee.
> Fain I would to Thee be brought,
> Gracious God, forbid it not.
> In the kingdom of Thy grace
> Give a little child a place.

As that quotation will suggest, my mother was an imaginative and sophisticated woman. She read eagerly and well. She wrote a beautiful hand, for which she was admired into old age, and she composed engaging letters. She wrote to me every day that I was in the army and once a week after I left England. She would have seemed to some obsessive, but her love was large and lavish. It took me years to understand how much it inhibited me. Only after I fled England did I come on Rainer Maria Rilke's reading of the parable of the prodigal son as a story of a man who fled an excess of love.

A friend of my mother's told me when I was an adolescent that my mother was the "most Christian woman" she had ever known. She was certainly a true believer and a devoted Methodist, giving herself to the chapel in one leadership role after another. She exhibited in her daily life the virtues Christians prize: generosity, kindness, devotion, love. But her strongly held conviction that Methodism was the "true" religion made her intolerant. She curled her lip at the Anglicans, who "went in for pomp and decorations," by which she meant ritual and clerical garb. But it was the Catholics she both scorned and feared, few as were their numbers in our village. There was no limit to her indignation when she talked of the "unnatural" celibacy of priests and nuns, of the Pope's wish to "take over England" again, or the large and underfed families that followed from the Pope's prohibiting birth control. Yet, once she saw that my friendship with Frank Kelly was deep and lasting, she welcomed him into our house as though he were English and a Methodist. Nevertheless, she remained haunted by the fear that I would fall for a Catholic girl and then be compelled to raise her (many) grandchildren as Catholics. I saved her from that, but did worse: I married an American.

My mother prided herself on being a woman of her word. She often told me about her mother's father, who owned a little shop in the village and was famous for holding to his word. On one occasion a man came into the shop and asked, "Do you have two shillings for a sixpence?" Caught off guard, Grandpa Robinson said "Yes," and only when he reached for his cash drawer did he realize that the man had tricked him into agreeing to what he thought was the opposite: two sixpences for a shilling. But he held to his word, giving the man the two coins even as he repeated his "Yes." But then he added, "Don't come in here again." That was the standard my mother set for herself and on at least one occasion I ruthlessly exploited it.

We had a little pantry beneath the stairs when we lived at 5 Blands Avenue and it housed the gas meter into which my mother had to put a shilling regularly to keep the gas flowing. One day when she went in to feed the meter I quickly closed the door and locked her in. Then I told her I would release her only if she promised to buy me a toy I wanted. My mother attempted to talk me out of it, eventually mentioning that she had to get tea ready for my father's expected arrival, and even resorting to asking me to get the woman next door to come so that she could talk to her about something. Five- or six-year old that I was, I saw through that one quickly. Finally and after a long time she agreed to my terms, to which I then added the demand that she not tell my father about my "trick" on her. She agreed, bought me the toy, but gave me a Grandpa Robinson-like rebuke and made me promise not to do anything of the sort again.

Having a next-door neighbor in for a cup of tea and a chat was a frequent thing with my mother. Her favorite activity was gossiping and there was nobody who could match her as a talker. As I grew older, I was endlessly amused by her constant denying that she liked to gossip and by the injured tone in which she would blame others for having too long engaged her. On her Saturday afternoon trips into Castleford to shop, she invariably took at least twice as long as she needed for her shopping. As tea-time approached and my mother failed to appear, my father would put the cloth on the table; a few minutes later he would set the table, all the while grumbling about my mother's tardiness. His last ploy was to fill the kettle and put it on the hearth to boil and that usually seemed to do the trick. For my mother would rush in, grabbing the kettle before she removed her hat and coat, and pour the boiling water into the teapot. Then while she disrobed she would account for her being late by saying, "They kept me talking." I think that is my favorite memory of her: that feigned innocence, the denial of blame, even while she named no particular party as the one guilty of holding her against her will.

My mother was much admired in the village and there have been scores of folk who have told me over the years that she was the best teacher they ever had. But there were some in the village who were at least amused by her putting on airs. Once when I was back on a visit a man a dozen years older than I—and I was then in my forties—called out in a mock high-pitched voice as

I passed the bench where he was sitting with his cronies, "Bruce, I'll smack your BTM." My mother could never bring herself to say "bottom" even indoors and "BTM" was her substitute that our former neighbor had remembered. She disliked intensely the "bum" that his mother would likely have used. I learned euphemisms from my mother long before I knew what a euphemism was.

Eva Street Haywood was the strongest and best influence on my life; to her I owe the "different" life I have led. She was, of course, pleased that I earned degrees from McGill and Harvard, though she never quite understood what moved me into German studies. That I taught she knew and applauded, but she was mystified by my activities as an academic administrator. I visited her not long after I had become President of Monmouth College and, when she inquired about what my new job entailed, I took her through a typical day in my office: meetings with my staff, with faculty members and their committees, talks with students individually and in groups, letters to trustees and alumni, preparing grant proposals to foundations, and all the hourly changes of gears that made my office exciting. She listened carefully and at the end said, "It sounds as though you don't do anything but talk and write to people." That didn't sound like real work to a Yorkshire woman.

It was a very profound shock to my mother that I became an American citizen, that I had, in her phrase, "renounced my birthright." That was being "different" in a degree she had never imagined and she never quite forgave me for it, not until, at least, years later she embraced her American granddaughters. She was very grateful that Gretchen and I had brought them to England to be christened in her chapel and, later, that my children talked of being "half English." They gradually conditioned her—as they did not my father—to take a more benign view of the United States and to be glad that her only son had found a rich life in America. I am certain that she never understood that she had put my infant foot on the path that led me here.

This remarkable vehicle was called a "charabanc." My parents are right by the first door after the windshield, on a vacation tour in a west coast seaside town, early nineteen-twenties, before I was born.

My father, on the right, with a 'twenties bus of the West Riding Company that employed him for most of his working life. His "conductor" took the money and issued tickets.

Chapter 5
What's In a Name?

Not long after my birth my mother walked me through the village in my new "pram," as the English call a baby carriage, doubtless on her way to her parents' house. (She always called that "going down home.") Somewhere along the way she was hailed by a woman who wanted to look at the new baby. "And what have you called him?" she wanted to know. Hearing "Bruce" she cried astonished, "Why, you've given him a dog's name!"

It has been one of history's patterns that conquerors take the names of the conquered's heroes for their pet dogs. (I had an American colleague in Germany just after World War II who named his dog Bismarck—and he didn't hail from North Dakota.) So it was with the English and their practice of calling their dogs after Scotland's greatest hero. My mother, for it was she who insisted on naming me, may have had some notion that we had a Scottish aristocrat in our family tree, perhaps a part of her never-ending wish that we be "different." In a village where most lads were called Jack, Tom, Dick, Fred, Bill, George—good solid English names all—mine was a name that marked me as an alien. I was in the British Army before I ever met another man named Bruce, and he a Scot; to that point the only Bruces I knew were dogs. I have sometimes wondered whether the sense of alienation that eventually drove me away from England began with my name. (I didn't have a middle name that I might have adopted to save me from the stares I inevitably encountered in England whenever I was called on to give my Christian name.) And was I first drawn to the boy who became my closest friend because he was cursed with being Francis Kelly? At least our parents were not attempting an elaborate joke on us, like the creator of the Lear jet, who named a daughter Crystal Shanda Lear.

There was more suffering to come. It was the practice of language teachers in English schools to give their pupils equivalent names for classroom use: Henri or Heinrich for Henry in French or German class, for example. On my very first day in French class in my new school, Miss Taylor went around the class, asking for first names and coming up with near equivalents. My "Bruce" stumped her, but after a minute of wrinkled brow she decided that a Scottish royal name demanded a French royal name and came up with "Louis." In German class I was "Bruno" and I could live with that. But Louis? That sounded just like the "Louie" my cousin Louise was called familiarly, a girl's name. One of my classmates said he proposed to date me. Was there no end?

Fortunately for Kelly and me, the English in those days hardly ever used first names. I went through seven years of prep school with boys whose first names I never learned; teachers called us by our family names. There I could be comfortable, for Haywood (a variant of Heyward, a Saxon derivative for a hedge or boundary guard), had an unmistakably English sound to it, while Kelly (who eventually managed to become Frank and thus nicely Saxon), still had to contend with being labeled Irish. He coped. Whereas there were no Bruces in all of Yorkshire, so far as my limited acquaintance took me, there were lots of Haywoods around, most of them my relatives. So even as my first name pushed me away from life's center, my family name pulled me towards it, an ambivalence that has characterized my life. Like Thomas Mann's Tonio Kröger, I have detested my origins even as I have passionately embraced them. Sometimes Allerton, the place I fled to find a larger world, seems to me the only real place I have ever known, its dialect the only true language I speak.

My name was bad enough; my nickname was worse. Allerton was a place of nicknames. There were so many Joes among the Prince families that nicknames were the only way of conveniently differentiating them. Thus there was a Big Joe, a Little Joe, a Happy Joe, and—believe it or not—a Sloppy Joe. Among my schoolmates were a "Titus" Oates and a "Turnip" Townshend, both after historical figures. For reasons I have never been able to guess, another was called "Cufflinks." There was a "Pops," a "Stosh," a "Rot," a "Champ." I came by my nickname because, once again, I was different.

In those days English boys were circumcised only if they could not, in my mother's explanatory phrase, "pass their water." That I was circumcised made me an object of curious interest to the village's older boys. I still shudder at the memory of them throwing me to the ground and one of them, in pre-zipper days, unbuttoning my fly to reveal my poor wounded member for their amusement. Invariably when they were done laughing, one of their number, as though to make me more aware that I was not like them, would spit on my foreskin-less penis before leaving me to my shame and my fly buttons. I raged helpless against them, vowing a revenge when I should reach their size. So inevitably in that place of identifying nicknames, I became "the little Jew." But as I grew larger that turned into a more friendly and rhyming "Juice." By that time I was about the tallest lad in the village and might have found a way to give my tormentors their lumps, but I never did. In the end it was easier to live as Juice than it was to live as Bruce. Or Louis.

My difference made me stay away from gang showers after games and stand very close to urinals. I'm confident that it contributed to the shyness that crippled my childhood and adolescence. Did it then play a part in my eagerly embracing America, the land of the circumcised?

Names were very much at play in England's class system, members of the aristocracy often having hyphenated names like Bowes-Lyon. Like many another practice, that has crept down into the lower classes since World War II. Among the upper class, family names were commonly of French origin, a continuing reminder of the Norman Conquest of 1066, while working class names often spoke to the job a serf ancestor performed: Smith, Cooper, Butcher, Miller, Butler. The aristocracy were also likely to give their offspring several first names; the present heir to the throne, Prince Charles, has half a dozen. That was a practice A.A. Milne mocked in one of the best of his "Pooh" poems, when he called a three-year-old James James Morrison Morrison Weatherby George Dupree. I thought my friend Kelly unusual in having a middle name, Joseph, until I learned that most Catholic children were like him in that respect. I never knew of Kelly or anybody else making use of a middle name, but then we rarely heard a first name being used. Some working class parents were obviously like my mother in choosing a name for a child that would push it towards the middle class. I knew a Sydney, a Clarence, a Douglas, but I never knew a dog to have one of those names.

More pointedly, families who had escaped public housing gave their houses names, some of them more than esoteric. I knew a "Journey's End," a "Mon Repos," a "Dun Roamin." A name on a house was a mark that the people living there owned their house—or at least had a mortgage on it. I was born in 2 Blands Grove and we lived subsequently in 5 Blands Avenue, row houses on streets in a "council housing estate." But when we moved to our own place, a "semi-detached villa," my parents named it

"Ventnor," that being the name of a town on the Isle of Wight that my father developed an affection for in his navy days. Our full post office address then was

> "Ventnor,"
>> Preston Lane,
>>> Allerton Bywater,
>>>> Near Castleford,
>>>>> Yorkshire, W.R.

spread across the face of the envelope in that fashion, still the English way. It was a very hard blow indeed to my mother when the government decreed that, in order to assist the post office to do its work, all properties must have a number. Names were no longer acceptable on letters. We had been dropped a rung on the social ladder!

My parents remained in "Ventnor" for over forty years, until my father's death. I flew over for his funeral in 1976 and found his coffin in what had once been called "the front room," standing before the piano he had given me my first lessons on. There was no longer a "front room," for my father, in what always seemed to me a smart and belated move, had had an arch cut between the living room and the front parlor, creating a much larger and open living area. But my mother had the sliding glass doors across the arch closed, she having never wanted the change. For that had meant letting go of the idea of a room that was always ready to receive visitors, neat, tidy, and polished. Even though those visitors hardly ever came. But having a front room that hadn't been turned into a barber shop or a fish shop was a middle class thing and my mother cherished that.

Chapter 6
Chapel Folk

The English, our newspapers have recently reported, continue to think of themselves, in the main, as Christians, yet under three percent attend a church. It was different in my childhood, when the majority were either "church" or "chapel" and Sunday services, morning and evening, were well attended. Even better attendance was at afternoon Sunday schools, to which were sent the children of both the regular church- and chapel-goers and those who had forsaken formal religion in order to be able to go to the pub. For to be a Methodist, at least in Yorkshire, meant being teetotal. Nothing, I rather suspect, has contributed more to the decline of mainstream religion in England than the belief that beer and faith could not co-exist. Nobody was more devoted to that conviction than my mother, who was never able to understand that there was a difference between "having a drink" and "drunkenness." I was lectured on the evils of drink almost as often I was urged to be a good boy, and those warnings certainly contributed to my postponing my first experiments with alcohol until I was into my early twenties.

There were plenty of examples of boozers in my village, whose names could be recited when I was being exhorted to stay away from public houses. Even as a small child I could recognize the damage being done to families whose fathers spent every evening "knocking back pints." Respecting my mother as I did, I never let her know that I had become an occasional drinker (I am barely that today), and when I visited her I never joined my friend Kelly in a pub that was close to Allerton or one that Allerton folk might frequent.

My first sense of what our being Methodists meant was that we were teetotal. The Haywoods and the Streets alike, or so it seemed to me as a child, were staunch in their rejection of alcohol. Years later I understood that there were some in both families who had become pub-goers, some even managing to remain chapel-goers as well. But when I was tiny the line seemed clearly drawn.

By the time I began school I had learned of another division, one that sometimes seemed, in my family's conversations, to be as important as that between teetotalers and pub-crawlers. That was the altogether fundamental difference between "church" and "chapel."

"Church" meant the Church of England, the established church which government funds and endowments supported, its future guaranteed. "Church" meant the presence of a vicar who resided in the village, in my youth in the person of Parson Bell. I sometimes glimpsed him as he walked to his church from his nearby residence and I saw him practicing his profession every Armistice Day. Then we children were marched to the nearby War Memorial, to sing hymns and to hear Parson Bell speak of those who had served in the Great War and pray for the souls of those who had given their lives for England. I was raised to believe that Parson Bell, no matter what his authority might be in the eyes of the King, did not speak for the true faith.

No, the true faith was ours; it was Methodism, it was "chapel." Being "chapel," I soon learned, meant a constant struggle to raise money, through the weekly collection plate and special "drives," just to keep the chapel open. I often heard my mother tell of two ladies of the chapel who were washing paint-work on the outside of the building, when two men passed by on their way home from the pub. One of them said in a loud voice to his fellow, "Am plannin' on bein' buried in t' chapel when ah dee (I die)." "Is tha then?" one of the ladies, outraged, cried. "An' who's tha think is goin' ter keep it oppen till tha's ready?" A lot of Street and Haywood money went into the building of that chapel and its maintenance. I have watched its congregation dwindling down since World War II and I must doubt that it can survive into another generation. In many a Yorkshire village the chapel, its congregation disappeared, has become a "walk around shop," as the English sometimes call a market.

Our chapel was a bare place, with little or no adornment. The interior walls were in the same brick as the exterior; there were no iconic figures; stained glass was visible, but there was not much of it; the floors were without carpet. Everything spoke of simplicity and frugality, the essential Yorkshire virtues. The pews seemed harder than any I have since encountered.

We were part of a "circuit" that centered on Castleford, where two ministers lived. They were "circuit riders," taking a bus to one village for morning service, to another for evening worship, so that we saw one or the other of them perhaps twice a month. At other services we had an unpaid "local preacher," a man or, rarely, a woman who came to us from Castleford or an area village. For me the chief difference between the professionals and the volunteers was one of accent and idiom. Whereas the ministers spoke standard English and avoided dialect words, the "locals" sounded just like us and were therefore the more understandable—and believable. But the happy constant in our services was the lusty singing of those great Methodist hymns. I sang some of them before I really understood their words. For instance, it was several years before I understood that "Rock of Ages, cleft for me" wasn't a plea that the Rock look after me. "Cleft" was not a part of my childhood vocabulary and I supplied a meaning that seemed to fit the hymn's sentiment. The first line of the preface to our hymn book ran, "Methodism was born in song" and I find that the Methodism that survives in me is mostly contained within the words of hymns like "Abide with me" and "Nearer my God to Thee." They were my first engagement with music and they contain the tenets of my belief. I married into the Presbyterian Church, which does not sing my favorite hymns, partly because it does not have evening services.

I seemed to spend most of Sunday at services or walking to and from them. (A Methodist prohibition on spending money on a Sunday meant that we took a bus only if the rain were very heavy.) We were in chapel from eleven to noon and again from six to seven-thirty. But in between I had an hour of Sunday School starting at two, so it was easy for me to believe that Sunday was indeed the Lord's Day. And every evening service was followed by a visit to my grandpa's, so that the day for me was one without playtime. My mother held me to that schedule until I was sixteen or so, when I was allowed to avoid going "home" with her. It was my first taste of the joys of adulthood.

Not surprisingly, my first childhood friendships were with boys from Methodist families. My first crush, when I was nine or so, was on Doreen Manley, a newcomer to the village who, despite her lovely Irish name, was English and Methodist. Years later I played the organ at her wedding and got paid for it. (If she hadn't snubbed me, I might have played for nothing. No, I'm too Yorkshire for that.)

So, long before I had a sense of being English or even Yorkshire, my first sense of a group identity was being Methodist. That meant that I distanced myself from the Anglicans, whom I was taught to suspect because of their near-papist ways. Only once did I enter the village church and that was when some sort of missionary was conducting a week of evening services that featured a "magic lantern" show of colorful slides, obviously the attraction for us who were not Anglican. I must have pleaded very persuasively and have pointed to other children whose Methodist parents had permitted them to go to earlier services. Only slowly did I overcome my suspicion of the Anglicans and play with "church" boys. But by then my friendship with Francis Kelly was about to blossom and that changed everything.

Looking back, I am surprised that my mother's class consciousness and desire to be thought above the ordinary did not lead her to abandon the chapel and embrace the church. (Though I recognize immediately that her loyalty to her father and her family would never have allowed her to do that.) It was early evident to me that the men of the chapel, with very few exceptions like my grandpa, my father, and Uncle George, were pit men, whereas the shopkeepers, the clerks at the mine, and the pit's under-managers were nearly all Anglicans.

If there was ever mention in my chapel years that Jesus Christ was Jewish, it was certainly played low key. As a small child I had no sense of there being Jews in the world, at least not in England. But eventually I was made aware of Jews who sold goods from stalls in Castleford's open-air marketplace on a Saturday afternoon. One of them, a woman with vocal chords like Ethel Merman's, sold pots and pans while keeping up a song-and-chatter act with the crowd around her stall. My mother would stop on the perimeter for a moment or two, watching and listening to "Pan Annie," but then she would pull me away and mutter something about the woman's vulgarity. I had found her immensely entertaining and I resisted being pulled away. Later my mother would refer to her as "that noisy Jewess in Castleford market" and tell me that Pan Annie came from Leeds every week and had been doing so for years. She would go on to explain that there was a colony of Jews in Leeds and that some Christians were paid to go to their homes on the Sabbath to light their fires, for devout Jews did no work whatsoever on the holy day. In my little mind that joined with our being prohibited from spending money on the Sabbath, something I resented bitterly because it meant that I could never have ice cream on a Sunday. So I felt a certain kinship in suffering with those Leeds Jews. Eventually I began to understand that there was a casual anti-Semitism in my family that translated into references to Jews being "not like us," "not really English," and I soon recognized that same easy rejection of Jews in most people I knew. Waiting my turn for a haircut when I was ten or eleven, I heard my barber-uncle declare, "What this country needs is a Hitler." Nodding heads around the room greeted his talk of getting rid of the parasitic Jews that were the ruin of England.

I was in the army before I met my first Jew, a fellow trainee in the Intelligence Corps, and we became friends. Coincidentally enough, he was from Leeds. Much later, after I had seen what Hitler's programs against the Jews resulted in, I began to wonder what would have happened in England, if the Germans had successfully invaded England in 1940, after the defeat of France. Would the English have been like the Danes, sheltering Jews at considerable risk to themselves, defiantly wearing a Star of David on a jacket as Jews were required to do? Or would the English have been like the French, collaborating with their German conquerors and rounding up Jews for shipment to the camps? I have reluctantly concluded, remembering all those casual denunciations of Jews that I heard for years, that it was likely that the English, by and large, would have been pleased to see the Jews go.

Until I got to know Frank Kelly and his two younger brothers I had no sense of there being Catholics in our village. That was partly because the Catholics were clustered at the west end of the village, partly because the Catholic kids went to parochial school in Castleford. But my mother had known of their presence in the village and in the country at large, she believing that the Pope was arranging for thousands of Irish people to move to England as part of his plot to reclaim England for the Vatican. As my friendship with Frank bloomed, I spent increasing amounts of time in the company of Catholic boys, and my other friends fell away. I was soon a regular visitor to the Kelly household, astonished at first by the number of holy figures and pictures about. The house actually belonged to Mrs. Kelly's uncle and the Kelly family lived rent free in return for feeding and looking after Uncle Pat, who with his brothers had come to England to work in the mines when they were young men. He was a dear old man, already retired from the pit when I first knew him, with an Irish brogue I learned to imitate. He grew fond of me and I always made a point of stopping to see him on my later visits to England, long after Frank and his brothers no longer lived there. The last time I saw him he was on his death bed, in the front room. He slowly made out my features as I bent over him and then he put up his hand to my face and said my name. "Are you still living in Canada, then?" he asked. Before I could explain that I had moved to the States, he went on, "You must keep an eye open for my brother Frank. He went to live over there, oh so many years ago. But you'd know him right away. He's a big fella."

As I grew older I recognized that there was an uncommonly large percentage of pretty girls among the Catholics, which I was slow to attribute to the fact that they were Irish. Mary Cairns, Veronica Conroy, Paddy McManus were in turn my crushes, if never my girlfriends. I can still see their pretty faces. Like the rest of us, the Irish children had become Yorkshire children and spoke the dialect with no trace of their parents' or grandparents' brogue.

A few years after I became part of the Catholic crowd, the Diocese built a small church just a few yards down the street from our house, much to my mother's chagrin, and my friends no longer had to go into Castleford for services. For a couple of years the new church was served by a priest from Castleford, but when the house next to the church came on the market it was purchased by the church for a resident priest. This greatly increased my mother's anxiety and she now saw the priest as a key figure in the planned Catholic take-over of all England. Nevertheless her Christian convictions led her to greet the priest whenever she encountered him on the street, though she would always wish to tell us afterwards that she could smell beer on him. For the priest was quickly at home in the local pub. Being my mother's child, it was not easy for me to come to understand that the priest was no less holy for having had an evening drink, even as it was not easy at first for me to understand that Mrs. Kelly, her chores for the day done, would go off to the pub with her sister. (Like many Yorkshire couples, the Kellys did their drinking in separate, but equal, pubs.)

It was in a field behind the row of houses where the Kellys lived that I first encountered Frank. Still new to the west end, I spotted a group of boys playing cricket and I was eager to join in. A couple of them already knew me from the village school and welcomed me. I was soon drawn to Frank, partly because he was the star player of the group, good enough that he became in time the best bowler in my school and a fast bowler for the county team. (As people in England do, he went on playing cricket well into middle age.) But he was better known to those of us who were his intimates as a devoted cigarette smoker; he became that when he was no more than nine years old. Outside a grocer's at the corner of our street was a slot machine where for one penny you could get one cigarette and one match. Kelly was a customer there whenever he had a penny, though his purchases exposed him to the risk that he would be seen and reported to his parents. They raged at him for his smoking and Uncle Joe Grainey, my favorite among his relatives, actually made him eat a pack of cigarettes to try to break him of the habit, after repeated washing of his mouth with laundry soap had failed to do it. Nothing worked.

Though I was a year ahead of him in school, Frank and I were inseparable for eight or nine years, our closeness ending with our war service and my early marriage. I always had a visit from him when I returned to England and the old spark of our friendship would unite us. Ours was in some ways an unlikely friendship, apart from our clan differences. Frank wasn't musical, I was not his equal as an athlete, we didn't read the same books or magazines. But we laughed at the same things and we laughed a lot. We were bonded, perhaps, in our sense of being odd and, besides, our upbringing made us virtuous. We were afraid of girls and we didn't seek fights with other boys. We became young socialists and enemies of the aristocracy. Without ever being bitter about it, we resented being among the working poor and near the bottom of the social order. We both had an early sense that we would wind up in teaching, if we survived the war. In the years of our adolescence survival seemed anything but certain.

*Members of the "Ladies Bright Hour" off for a day at the seaside.
My Dad is the driver; my Mother took the photograph.*

Here, I am going on five and weeping because I have been obliged to "lay a brick" for the new Sunday School in memory of my paternal grandparents.

Chapter 7
Forever Shy

The question raised its ugly head every year of my childhood: Was I going to recite a poem this year at the Sunday School Anniversary?

It was the practice at the Allerton Methodists to have certain special Sunday afternoon occasions when particular groups strutted their stuff. (Like so many things that went on at the chapel, the real object was to raise money through a special collection.) Thus the members of the "Ladies Bright Hour," a group of women who met on Wednesday for afternoon tea and an uplifting talk (more often than not from my mother), would perform an annual cantata. The choir would have its day, another occasion for a cantata. The men's group would perform its cantata, and that meant an afternoon of particularly bad singing. There were but a few good voices in our congregation and only two or three of those were male. Then there was the Harvest Festival, when the chapel was decorated with sheaves of wheat and the altar rail and the pulpit were adorned with fruits of various shapes, sizes, and colors; this too was the occasion for a cantata. I have heard more than my share of simple narratives punctuated by solos and choral numbers that seemed to have only passing reference to the text. Or to music.

But the date on the chapel calendar that filled me with dread was that of the Sunday School Anniversary. This occasion was ostensibly to celebrate the umpteenth birthday of the building adjacent to the chapel, constructed several years after the chapel's being built. I have a photo of me "laying a brick" in memory of my paternal grandparents, their names chiseled into the brick's surface. I was only four when I was pressed into that duty and, inevitably, I was crying when the photograph was taken. I was weeping because I was so miserably shy that doing anything before other people reduced me to tears. And that was the problem with the Sunday School Anniversary.

It was an occasion, not for yet another cantata, mercifully, but for the performance by kids from two to fourteen of little songs and poems. Every year my Sunday School fellows took their places on the platform erected over the altar for the event, dressed in their best, all hair-curled and shiny-faced, and did their thing. They did it with no nerves showing, no embarrassment, no bowel problem. They knew that, out there in the pews somewhere, their parents, grandparents, uncles and aunts, sisters and brothers were watching, and yet they stood up and performed their piece. Smiling, happy, self-confident. I didn't. I skulked in the Street family pew, an annual embarrassment to my parents, grandparents, etc., etc., because it was obvious that once again I had been unable to bite the bullet. I just couldn't do it.

My mother didn't want me to be shy—not that kind of different, Bruce—because she knew it would limit my opportunities. So she insisted that I wasn't. She accused me of being coy, playing games, trying to get attention, goodness knows what. But not shy. "Look at all the other children; you can do it as well as they can." Then it was "obstinate, selfish, uncaring." In due time I was offered threepence, a year later sixpence, if only I would do just one little four-line poem. We never got to a shilling, though even that wouldn't have made a difference. The problem was that I was scared of having to stand before a group of people and expose myself to their scrutiny. For me, it was that simple. For my mother, even early on, the question was, how was I ever going to become a Methodist minister, if I couldn't address an audience? Well, I wasn't. I resigned myself to having to go down the pit.

I endured the yearly wooing and cajoling, even the attempts at bribery, and held my ground. I had to endure the taunts of classmates, too, for I had to give them some explanation for my not standing shoulder to shoulder with them on the great day But the years passed, if slowly, and I ended my Sunday School career with no runs, no hits, and no errors. Some of my classmates had a lot of errors, sometimes forgetting the last couple of lines of their poem or singing badly off key. To this day I cannot see mention of Rudyard Kipling without thinking of the many manglings of his poem "If." Nobody minded. It was the being-up-there on the platform that counted. "Look, that's our Joyce. Doesn't she look lovely?"

That "our" was another Allerton thing. There were so many Joes, Marys, Bills in the village that, in order to make absolutely clear that it was the Joe, Mary, or Bill of their family they were talking about, people said "our Joe" or "our Mary" or "our Bill." Or they would say "your Joe" if they were referring to their companion's family member of that name. The practice was such a habit that I, who was unique in the village, was called either "our Bruce" or "your Bruce" as the context demanded. Of course, that did prevent any confusion with somebody else's dog.

I did not grow out of my shyness; indeed, it is with me today. Over the years it has caused me to shrink from social and even professional opportunities. It was a barrier in my relations with what we used to call the fair sex. I had my crushes from afar until I fell in love for the first time.

Molly Dibb was a year behind me in school and I first became aware of her when she was in the fifth form and I in the Lower Sixth. By then I was a prefect, an office which had few duties attached to it, but a considerable amount of prestige. The prefects' chief responsibility was to line up the classes at the morning assemblies and to hush any child who might be causing a ruckus—a rare thing indeed. I found myself responsible for 5A, Molly's section of the fifth form, a class in which I had a couple of rugby team pals, but that was otherwise *terra incognita*. My role required me to serve first as the point on which the class members lined up and then to remain there on the side during the assembly, in case 5A suddenly decided to break ranks. In the course of the year I took to gazing on

Molly with an increasing appreciation of her charms, but with no notion that I would ever approach her. Mine was a school where there were taboos against interactions between boys and girls and I would have suffered at least a rebuke, if a teacher had caught me gazing. But I watched Molly discreetly through the winter and spring, never detecting a returned look from her. In truth, with the balancing act I was doing with my school work and my piano playing I had no thought of advancing our relationship beyond my appreciative looks.

But in September, when school opened again, and I found Molly, along with other members of Lower Sixth Arts, sharing classroom space with us Upper Sixth Arts types, it seemed as though fate were drawing us together. I felt the pulse quicken, the blood course in the veins. Thoughts began to stir in me of my violating the school's code and my parents' notions of what was proper for me; I began to think of asking Molly to go to the movies with me some Friday evening. That was what we imagined big-time dating to be; it was all we had ever heard of. In our little world couples went to the movies a few times, he walked her home, and after a few months of this they kissed goodnight and then they got married.

But my shyness stood between Molly and me, knotting my tongue, making me blush when we found ourselves approaching a door together. Finally I confessed my interest in her to one of my pals in her class and asked him to mediate. Molly seemed not surprised by this approach and she let me know, when we nearly ran into each other later in the day, that she would be willing to receive an invitation for the very next Friday. Whoopee, joy overflowing.

I imagine that the knowledge that we were sampling forbidden fruit lent a certain spice to our dating. We knew that we both might suffer suspension or even expulsion, if one of our teachers happened to see us in the movie theater or walking together on the street. (The wartime blackout was our ally; it was impossible to see anybody after dark.) The only school couple who seemed to make no effort to hide their relationship, which began in the fourth or fifth form, Charlie Stenner and Dorothy Shaw, were caught in the movie by no less a person than the headmaster himself. As luck would have it, he and his wife took seats right behind them. Once Mr. Hampson's eyes grew accustomed to the dark of the theater and he identified the couple as pupils of his, he ordered them to the lobby. He held Stenner there until he thought Dorothy would be safely home and then released him, with orders for the two of them to be in his office after the assembly on Monday morning. He expelled the two of them when they admitted that this was far from their first offense, but eventually he reinstated them after their parents visited his office and made clear that their children had their blessing and that the relationship was a serious one. Indeed it was; a few years later they married and lived happily ever after.

Not so, Molly and I. I knew after a few months of very limited hand holding in the movie and even more limited goodnight kisses at her door, that I was in love with her. I never told her that, luckily enough, for, although she was "my girl" until I went into the army, she let me know in a brief letter a couple of months later that she was playing the field. I did not collapse in tears, but shrugged my shoulders and soldiered on. We were to meet again, to our mutual surprise, when I was home on leave from Germany and visiting Castleford with my cousin Malcolm (then fourteen or so). I ran into her on a shopping street, she by then a teacher in a local school. We chatted for a moment or two, engaging in some banter, and I knew for sure that it had not been love, after all. Malcolm was acutely embarrassed by the whole exchange.

It saddens me to write of Molly, fond as I am of the memory of her. Her family's history is a tragic one, but I must tell it.

Before the war there was a craze in our area for dog racing. Miners and others bought themselves greyhounds and whippets that they trained to pursue the mechanical hare and then they entered them at the Castleford track. I heard talk of large wagers, dangerous betting, and huge sums of money being paid for pups. (My parents, needless to say, were appalled by the whole business, particularly the betting.) Some of the owners took to training their dogs in Castleford's public park, to the anger of those who liked to walk their pet dogs there, and occasionally a greyhound would break loose and run off into the town. So it was that one day Mr. Dibb, working in his garden, saw a greyhound run into a neighbor's yard and there attack a little terrier, crushing it in its jaws. Mr. Dibb got over the fence and hit the greyhound on the head with his spade. The dog dropped dead. The damages awarded the greyhound's owner in his lawsuit bankrupted Mr. Dibb, forcing him to sell his little shop. He died not long after, a broken man. Worse was to come.

My friend Kelly married Molly's younger sister Margaret and they enjoyed a few idyllic years together, blessed with children, until Margaret died of cancer at only forty-one. Frank never remarried. Just a few years later Molly met the same fate, she too leaving behind a husband and young children.

My shyness continued to plague me and in truth it has never left me, though I have nearly mastered the art of disguising it, to the degree in fact that people scoff at me when I claim to be bothered by it. As they do when I speak of my stage fright.

Even as I avoided the stage of the Sunday School Anniversary, so did I avoid any stage that people tried to put me on in my school days, except for my one and only appearance as a jazz authority. (Passion for the subject and missionary zeal got me through that.) But there came the day when I had to go before my first class of Harvard undergraduates. I got not a minute of sleep the night before and I was a nervous wreck when I entered the classroom. After the ordeal was over and the class hour at an end, I comforted myself with the thought that I would certainly outgrow my stage fright. I didn't. Every new course I taught at Harvard and subsequently at

Kenyon meant that I had to face the same first frightening minutes, when I feared that I might become tongue-tied. When I became Kenyon's Dean the problem became acute, for I was called on to speak to large audiences of parents, alumni, or visitors to the College, to say nothing of my faculty and staff colleagues. Now I found the cramped stomach and dry mouth lasting and worsening as my address wore on. Close friends gave me their sympathy, but eventually I sought help from Paul Newman's teacher, my colleague Jim Michael. He tried to reassure me by telling me that even Laurence Olivier had stage fright, but his strong recommendation was that I stop reading from a script. Far better, he said, to speak as though I were before a class, using only a few notes. I took his advice and found myself able to cope with my problem, more or less.

It's rather nice to think that I was taught by the same man who taught Paul Newman all he knows. One thing I'm certain of: Mr. Newman and I have the same deep affection for the late Jim Michael, one truly worthy of the name "gentleman and scholar." He was one of Kenyon's best and he demonstrated his thoughtfulness convincingly when Paul Newman was on the Kenyon campus for an extended stay.

It happened because we of the administration made a serious error of judgment. In our planning in the nineteen-sixties for the great expansion of Kenyon and its move to coeducation, we worried over the amount of money we were going to have to raise for new buildings and facilities. But we never fretted a moment about where the million dollars for the new theater would come from. Paul Newman's affection for Jim Michael was well known and understood; it seemed certain that he would want his beloved teacher to have the facility he needed. And so, when the time came for the part of our construction program that included the new theater, the President of the College and Jim Michael headed off to visit good old Paul in Connecticut. They returned empty handed; Paul Newman's money was tied up in his children's prep schools and his newly formed production company. But he had promised to take the lead role in the first play produced in the new theater.

It took us a long time to raise the money for that theater, so long that by the time it was built the cost had risen to two million and Mr. Newman was not interested in acting on the stage. But he promised to direct the first play and so he came to spend a few weeks in

Gambier. Indeed, he was our next door neighbor, something I have dined out on quite a lot. Jim Michael, a widower by then, generously undertook to invite small groups of his colleagues and spouses to dine with Paul Newman of an evening. (I never heard of anybody in that self-consciously sophisticated and often cynical community turning down the opportunity.) And so my wife and I found ourselves one evening seated across from that famous face. Mr. Newman was a gracious table companion and I wasn't at all shy.

My stage fright is always with me. When I entered a Kenyon classroom for the last time, in 1980, to teach the course on Thomas Mann I had taught a half dozen times before, I suddenly panicked. As the last students arrived and took their places, I found myself, with stomach cramps crippling me, ready to tell them that I had suddenly been taken ill and must go home to bed. I was within an ace of doing it, but I swallowed hard and got under way.

I keep on accepting invitations to talk to service clubs and the like, always kicking myself when the club president is introducing me. Shyness, stage fright—two sides of the same coin. I should have licked the problem when I had the chance to get sixpence for doing it and could have had my parents beaming, like little Joyce's. "Look, that's our Bruce up there, ready to say his poem. It'll be the making of him." Who knows, it might have been.

Chapter 8
English Spoken Here, Sort Of

For a few years after I left England my mother insisted on sending me the local paper that was published weekly in Castleford, she believing that I would wish to keep up with news of my school friends. In truth, there was rarely an item of interest to me, my friends having left the area. One week, however, my attention was captured by a headline that announced the death of Allerton's oldest inhabitant, Tom Stoker, who had lived into his late nineties. He had seemed to me an old man when I was still a child and I remembered his presence among those retired miners who sat out on a bench smoking and talking.

What had really captured the interest of the reporter was the fact, revealed by his daughter, that Tom Stoker had spent every night of his life under the same roof, a fact the reporter trumpeted as though it were the accomplishment of a lifetime's labors. The whole village was proud of that record, he claimed. Tom's being a miner had exempted him from military service in two wars, helping to keep his unbroken string intact, and he had evidently been content to spend his vacations in the village. He had, to be sure, taken occasional day trips to the seaside, thirty miles or so away, but he had always returned to his own bed at day's end. At the time of his death there were four generations of his family under that same roof.

Nothing of this really surprised me. When I was a child there were two and three generations living in the same dwelling all over the village; it was the only way some of our people could cope in the Depression years, particularly if one or other of the husbands was a pub regular. And I'm confident that there were other elderly men and women who, though they might not be able to equal Tom's unbroken string, could come within an ace of it. For I knew many of whom it was said that they "never set foot outside Allerton." There were many, many others who, like my parents, spent all their lives in the village and were away from it never more than one week at a time, and that for an annual vacation at Scarborough or Bridlington, popular Yorkshire seaside resorts, where they were overjoyed to encounter other Allerton folk. My parents, returning from such a week with sticks of the traditional rock candy as presents for family members, invariably reported, as though incrementally measuring the success of their vacation, the names of fellow villagers they had met on the beach or on the promenade.

Though my mother might occasionally complain, particularly in her later years, that they "had never gone anywhere or seen anything," she seemed as sure as my father, who had to be pried out of the village, that there was no better place for Tom Stoker to have spent his many nights than Allerton Bywater. Nobody was more certain of that than I was in my adolescent years, for Allerton seemed the only stable place in a world that was drastically changed by the war and the years that led up to it.

My mother was usually willing to grant that other parts of Yorkshire had their attractions, even though she wasn't willing to live in any of them, but she never had a good word for anywhere outside Yorkshire. On one of my visits, after she had once again shaken her head over my having chosen to give up all that Allerton could offer in exchange for a life among the gangsters and Red Indians, I asked her whether she thought there might be anything anywhere that might be superior to its Yorkshire equivalent. She paused for a moment and then said that her youngest sister, who had by then traveled on the Continent, had reported that there was more sunshine in Italy. But my mother concluded that too much sunshine was probably not good for one. She liked

Yorkshire weather. The chill rain was good for women's complexions.

Yorkshire folk often described themselves as "clannish," though others might have said "chauvinistic." Clearly we believed Yorkshire to be the best part of England, Yorkshire people the salt of the earth. Others, we knew, thought us thickheaded, tight-fisted, stubborn, morose, suspicious, and xenophobic. Our adjectives for ourselves, instead, would have been thoughtful, thrifty, persistent, introspective, careful, and cautious for the time. These traits we might have attributed to our growing up in a harsh environment, to our Viking ancestors, and certainly to our having long been the butt of jokes made about us by Londoners. Clearly, outsiders didn't really understand or appreciate us and we accepted that as our lot.

A chief reason for others not being able to understand us was our dialect. Yorkshire, as we simply called it—or "broad" Yorkshire, if it were spoken without any concession to others—is a variant form of English that, resisting the French influences after 1066, has preserved many elements of the older forms of the language. Its consonants and pure vowels are so much like those of the part of Germany whence came the Angles and Saxons that, once I was fluent in

German, I was able to pass as a Bremen native by employing my Yorkshire speech sounds. Like German again, Yorkshire speech employs much more breath and vigor than standard English; we are often guilty of spraying others when we speak. Our vowels are often short, when in standard English they are long and diphthong. Aitches are nearly always dropped, as is the final g in present participles. There are, of course, certain words and phrases that are peculiar to Yorkshire, leaving outsiders baffled: a chicken house is called "t'en 'oyl," unwed cohabiters are said to be "livin' gormless." But the dialect's best feature for me has always been its retention of the familiar Germanic form of the second person pronoun, variously pronounced "tha,""thu," "thi," "thee," depending on the locality and the grammatical case. I do not ever recall hearing it pronounced "thou." Its use affords speakers a wonderful intimacy and I have always thought standard English impoverished by its having "you" serve both singular and plural forms.

Brevity is considered a very great virtue in Yorkshire; people are suspicious of the verbose. With characteristic self-deprecation, the essential Yorkshire virtues are proposed in this rhyme I learned as a child. (Yorkshire exists only as an oral form, so the text below is my effort at transcribing its sounds, with translations in parentheses.)

> Ear awl, see awl, say nowt.
> (Hear everything, see everything, say nothing.)
> Eight awl, sup awl, pay nowt.
> (Eat everything, drink everything, pay for nothing.)
> An' if ivver tha duz owt fer nowt,
> (And if ever you do anything for nothing,)
> Awluss doo it fer thi'sen.
> (Always do it for yourself.)

Now, there are Yorkshire people who would wish to insist that they have never used the dialect and have always spoken standard English. I cannot imagine the actress Judi Dench, growing up the daughter of a physician in the city of York, ever speaking it. The dialect is clearly the more used and cherished in villages and towns than in cities, though one hears it in Leeds and Sheffield, but in truth it is class status or class-consciousness that often determines whether or not a person uses the dialect. To some, obviously, the dialect will seem merely uncouth, the language of the uneducated plebeians. By the time my parents saw me off on the train to Worcester, where I would do my primary army training, I had come to recognize that the dialect, much as

I cherished it, was a trap. I should never escape my origins if I clung to its use. So I silently vowed, waving goodbye, that I would henceforth use only standard English and rid myself of all the traits that would identify me as a dialect speaker. I never quite made it and I have long since ceased trying. Nobody would ever confuse my "butter" with "putter," my "do" with "too."

I was gone from England for eight years before I returned. When we got off the train in Leeds and the vowels and consonants of the people on the platform fell on my ears, it was like a warm embrace reaching out to me. And so it has been on every visit subsequently. It is the mother's lap to which I have wanted to return in hard times, the smile of my best friend, the echo of a thousand happy moments. Once in a while I dream in the dialect and I awake astonished that I have not forgotten any part of it.

I can summon up the dialect and a host of Yorkshire memories by singing the county's "national anthem" to myself. Yorkshire's much loved song is called "Ilkla Moor 'baht 'at," in standard English "Ilkley Moor without a hat." That line, accompanying each question or statement put, is repeated over and over as a refrain to the many verses. Ilkley Moor, everybody in Yorkshire knows, is a very cold place indeed, so a swain who goes courting up there bare-headed is asking for his "death of cold." There are consequences to such folly!

Wier ess ter bin sin' ah saw thee?
(Where have you been since last I saw you?)
On Ilkla Moor 'baht 'at.
(On Ilkley Moor with no hat.)
Tha's bin a-courtin' Mary Jane,
(You've been courting Mary Jane,)

(Refrain, sung triumphantly!)
Tha's bahn to git thi dee-eth a cauwd,
(You are going to catch your death of cold,)
Then we s'll 'ave ter bury thee,
(Then we shall have to bury you,)
Then t'wums 'll cumm 'n eight thi up,
(Then worms will come and eat you up,)
Then t'ducks 'll cumm 'n eight up t'wums,
(Then ducks will come and eat up the worms,)
Then we s'll cumm 'n eight up t'ducks,
(Then we shall come and eat up the ducks,)
 Then we s'll awl 've etten thee!
(Then we shall all have eaten you!)

No rational explanation can be offered as to why this peculiar text with its happy and lusty tune has so captured Yorkshire people, who sing it endlessly at county football matches and similar occasions, always knowing its absurdities and its self-mockery. Why was it ever adopted in the first place? Why would Yorkshire folk sing it so merrily, knowing that others will ridicule them for it? I have read that soldiers charged German pillboxes singing that song. I know that I cannot hear it sung without getting a lump in my throat.

In the song's simple evocation of the cycle of life and death in a harsh world I find the essential Yorkshire recognition that life is very hard. Yorkshire is a place where people have sought to farm on cruelly sparse soil, where they have faced an uncertain, never friendly climate, where death was always somehow just around the corner, and where people recognized that their gain was very likely a neighbor's loss. But I have come to find in its astonishing popularity, as I have found in the persistence of the dialect itself against all odds, a declaration of defiance of those who would look down on Yorkshire folk. The crowds who sing "Ilkla Moor" sing it with pride. Acceptance of place, yes, but defiance of class condescension.

Nothing more defines English, and therefore Yorkshire, life than its layered social order, with the monarch and the aristocracy at the top, beneath that stratum a wealthy and privileged upper class that has no claim to purple blood, a relatively small middle class of professional persons, and a very large and impoverished working class. This medieval order has persisted into the present day with all of its viciousness intact. It will survive, presumably, so long as the English wish to go on being ruled, being subjects rather than citizens, being content to accept their place in what they see as a predestined system.

Now there are those today who will argue that the class system has disappeared, that people are able to rise to the level their talents can carry them. In some respects this is true—there are many more universities than there were before WWII, for example—but every contemporary English novel I read, every English film I see, tells me that class is still the ruling element in English life. People are so used to it that they are able to deny its existence. As recently as July, 2006 a columnist in an English newspaper took the Prime Minister to task for his having proposed that the government purchase a private jet for his official travel. This, the columnist said, was quite inappropriate; the Prime Minister should not wish to elevate himself in this fashion. Ours, he went on, is an egalitarian society; we are all equally the Queen's subjects. The irony obviously escaped him.

The class system has the monarchy as its corner stone; without the monarchy the system would soon collapse. Queen Elizabeth's face is the one most often seen on English television, on the front page of newspapers, on the covers of magazines. And every time English children see Her Majesty they get a subliminal message that what really counts in England is who your parents were. For the Queen was not elected to her office; she did not earn it; she was not chosen by her peers; she is Queen because her father was King, as was his father before him. It isn't long before English children also learn that the Princes, Dukes, Earls, Lords who are above them similarly inherited their places in the scheme of things, not to be dislodged by indolence, incompetence, or boorishness. It will come to seem inevitable to the children of the working class that they will inherit places in the bottom tier and, indeed, chances are slim that anybody will find it possible to move from the one stratum to the other—in either direction. The coal miner who wins the national lottery may suddenly be worth millions, but he will not find himself admitted to the London clubs of the upper class. But neither will the aristocrat who loses the family fortune at the casino in Monaco lose his place in the House of Lords, England's Senate. "There'll always be an England" the popular song proclaimed in World War II (to the annoyance of the Scots, Irish, and Welsh who were also fighting the enemy), and it is certain to be the England of the class system, so long as the monarchy survives.

What virtually guarantees the survival of the monarchy is the enthusiasm for it among the working class. For most of them, support for the monarchy is the equivalent of patriotism; it is treason to oppose it. It is among the educated middle class that the advocates of republicanism are to be found and they are still a minority. I was raised in a family of patriots and monarchists, at least one of my aunts being a near fanatic. She told me on many an occasion that the Queen was "the hardest working person in England" and she would tolerate no criticism of her, even in the days after the death of Princess Diana when the Queen's seeming indifference angered many Britons. In my aunt's early days in teaching, she made a practice of pointing out on a map of the world, prominently displayed on her classroom wall, all the parts of the British Empire. Then she would tell the children, "All those places in red are ours." After WWII, when the Empire ceased to exist and there were few places left on the map that might remotely be called "ours," she became paranoid, convinced that there was an international plot to strip away whatever was left of Britain's possessions and, eventually, to take over all of Britain. "First they'll take Gibraltar," she would intone, "then it'll be the Channel Islands one by one, and before we know it they'll be coming up the Ouse." I was never able to get from her who she believed the "they" were, though she often seemed to imply that the Americans were behind it.

What is it, I have wondered, that causes working class people to cling so tenaciously to the class system? I have concluded that it provides them with a sense of having a predictable place in their world, a feeling of security that comes with knowing what and where they are, a claim on being in a society that has an exalted monarch at its top. Easier to be a "subject," with the feeling that somebody at the top cares about them than being a "citizen" and having to be responsible for the society. But perhaps, in Yorkshire at least, it is simply a fondness for things remaining as they are. I know that feeling well.

Chapter 9
Yorkshire Pudding

Just as the Finns have sent but one concept out into the wide world—the sauna—so have Yorkshire folk given the world but one product of their genius: Yorkshire pudding. I cringe as I write that, for I have had set before me in this country, both in private homes and restaurants, something given the name "Yorkshire Pudding" that bore very little resemblance to the proper article. Honesty demands that I acknowledge that the same thing happened to me at my mother's table on occasion, for my poor mother, who never met a recipe she didn't ignore, produced some versions which were barely edible. To be fair to her, I must point out that she did her puddings in an oven which derived its heat from an open coal fire, a heat source not much more predictable than a candle, so she was able to blame both her burned-to-a-crisp version and her hopelessly undercooked version on the oven. She simply looked helplessly puzzled at those puddings that, while properly cooked, tasted peculiar. Rarely did she produce a pudding that was just right—and she a Yorkshire woman through and through—and that, I believe, happened because her guesses at proportions of flour, salt, and whatever, just happened to be right. It has been a thing of wonder to me that my mother's recipe began "Take one or two eggs." One *or* two? My American wife, on the other hand, who never met a recipe she didn't follow meticulously, invariably produced Yorkshire pudding fit for a king, though using an electric oven. So good is Yorkshire pudding when thus properly prepared and soaked in beef and onion gravy that I have made a whole meal of it, not desiring meat to go with it. It was initially, in fact, a dish for poor families, something to satisfy the hungers of the children so that they would be full by the time meat appeared on the table. Some of the best peasant food in the world had similar origins. Never did I know Yorkshire pudding to be served in Yorkshire as an accompaniment to the meat course, as it is everywhere else; it was always the first course and, for me, the best.

The pudding that I consider the authentic Yorkshire item is cooked in a large square pan, beginning as a yellowish-white liquid which rises under heat to about a half-inch thickness, richly browned and yet not crisped. It is served hot, straight from the oven, with rich onion gravy poured on it. My mouth waters, my nose twitches at the thought of it. The Yorkshire pudding I have been offered in this country has always been a popover of indeterminate shape and flavor, this to accompany roast beef. I have never enjoyed it. Fortunately, no hostess has ever asked me whether I liked my Yorkshire pudding, not even one who knew my Yorkshire origins, for the Yorkshire pudding of North America is no more associated with my native county than the sauna is with Finland.

So we are left with the Yorkshire terrier to give us a hook on which to hang our claim to recognition, and that cute little dog is about as un-Yorkshire as an animal could be: tiny, friendly, well behaved, and eager to please.

Next to Yorkshire pudding my favorite Yorkshire food was fish and chips, and that is a dish we cannot lay exclusive claim to, for it is a favorite in many parts of England. But I, who have eaten fish and chips in many places in England and elsewhere, would insist that the fish and chips of my Allerton childhood set the standard against which all others had to be measured. We Allerton folk were immensely fond of fish and chips (I might write those three words as one, so indissolubly joined are they), and I readily count five shops in my village where only fish and chips were fried, some of them in what had been originally the front parlor of the house. Nearly always a ma–and–pa operation, a fish shop sometimes saw the adolescent children of the family working in the shop, but whether or not the children helped out, their clothes were saturated with the smell of cooking fat. Like their parents, those children could never disguise the fact that they lived behind or above a fish shop.

With the North Sea and its riches so close to us, there was always a good supply of fish to be had, even in the early years of the war. At the fish shop "fish" meant cod, while "tail" meant haddock, a far less popular and more expensive item. "Chips" meant potatoes peeled and sliced large, deep fried in very hot fat that sizzled and popped as the potato slices were dropped in; our french fries are a poor substitute. So intense is the relationship of fish and chips for me, out of my childhood, that I have never been able, as an adult, to eat potatoes with fish in any form other than fried.

Fish'n'chips, whether consumed at noon or in late evening, was a staple in Allerton. It was also the lowest priced meal available outside the home. On Saturday mornings when I was a boy I would run a few errands for my grandma, for which she rewarded me with a sixpenny coin, a shiny silver piece about the size of a dime. That I carried to the nearest fish shop where, for two pence, I could get the children's special: a small fish and a little helping of chips. Two other pennies were reserved for my bus fares and the final two went for admission to the afternoon show at one or other of the movie theaters in Castleford. Like most children, I ate my fish'n'chips with my fingers, rolling back the newspaper that was wrapped about a sheet of wax paper that actually held the fish'n'chips. When we had fish'n'chips at home my mother insisted that they be eaten from a plate, using a knife and fork. I could never understand such a make-work activity, particularly when I was required to do the dishes afterwards.

There were, of course, people who made their own fish'n'chips, buying raw cod in Castleford market and using their home-grown potatoes, but frying chips was a dangerous venture and I knew three or four Allerton children who had been scalded with boiling fat from the chip pan. One girl was so disfigured that she had to have extensive plastic surgery. My mother, when frugality gripped her or when she was led to believe that home-fried chips were better than those the

Gledhill family produced, would give us broiled fish and her version of chips. The fish was often very good, particularly when it was plaice.

A particular favorite of mine was what my mother called "scallops," though hers had nothing whatsoever to do with shellfish. Rather, her scallop was a slice of potato dipped in batter and deep fried. It was a creature somewhere between a fried fish and a chip, the batter the best part. I didn't often get scallops, whether because my mother recognized the danger of frying them or because they were messy to make I do not know. I was given them as a special treat and I always was grateful to get them.

When I started reading American comics I was immensely puzzled as to what fried chicken was. It was something I simply could not imagine. For one thing, in our vocabulary a chicken was what Americans would call a chick and I couldn't think that anybody would fry one of those little balls of fluff. We called a chicken a hen and our first interest in a hen was that it was an egg layer. Only when it reached the age that it ceased to lay did a hen become an edible object and by then it was a tough old bird, fit only to be stewed. And even after my mother had stewed a chicken for hours, she would complain about its toughness and lack of flavor. I was several years an adult before I knew chicken in any other form, but when I first tasted fried chicken I knew what all the fuss was about. I justify my reckless consumption of it now by telling myself that I am making up for lost years. Yet I remember the chicken stews of my childhood fondly and I do not scorn chicken in any form now.

For a cold Yorkshire meal there was nothing as good as pork pie or sausage rolls, nothing as bad as tongue. The last, which my mother in her later years invariably called "beast's tongue," was the tongue of a cow marinated and boiled. It came in round slices, dense and dark red, off–putting in its appearance before its taste. I always insisted on eating it with HP sauce, the strong flavor of which was nearly enough to drown out the taste of the tongue. Only hunger made me eat it in my childhood and, on visits in my adulthood, I tried to convince my mother not to buy it. But, even as she could never remember that I drank my tea without milk or sugar, she never seemed able to remember that I disliked tongue. She was persuaded that it was a very healthy food and I think, moreover, that she liked its taste, so she frequently welcomed my daughters and me with the announcement that she had a "beast's tongue" all ready to take with us up the Dale.

How very pleasant, in contrast, it was to return to England and have an afternoon tea that featured pork pie. The English, and Yorkshire people particularly, like meat pies, as the omni-present steak and kidney pie, visible on every restaurant menu, gives evidence. Whereas that pie is always served hot, pork pie is best cold. Though it comes in several sizes, its shape is always the same: round and upright. Its crust is thick and absorbent, at its center one finds ground, cooked and flavored pork. The hostess serves wedges of it, often with a salad. In my youth there was a style of men's hat called a "pork pie," evidence of the well-known shape and popularity of the real object.

An alternative at tea-time was having a couple of sausage rolls, which were sausage meat inside puff pastry. Good ones melted in the mouth and left a happy memory. During the war bad sausage rolls, sometimes the only fare in railway station canteens, became a national joke and a guessing game as to their content. I have seen versions of the sausage roll at cocktail parties in this county—a tiny frank wrapped in dough—but, tasty as they are, they pale alongside the sausage rolls of my memory.

The English and the Americans, divided by a common language, certainly divide on the meaning of the word "sausage." The sausage of North America has a German forebear; it is solid meat. The English sausage has a cereal content flavored with meat, sometimes beef, more often pork. During World War II the government limited the cereal content to, as I recall, eighty-five percent; I have wondered whether our butcher dropped the content much below that after the war was over. Now, I must hasten to add that I loved English sausage, cereal and all, particularly when it came in the form of tomato-flavored pork sausage made by my childhood friend, Cliffie Prince. Cliff apprenticed himself to a local butcher when he left the village school at fourteen, serving mostly in his first years as the delivery boy, riding a bike around the village with wrapped orders in a basket in front. Later he learned to kill and cut, eventually taking over the business when the owner retired after WWII. My wife and daughters learned to love Cliffie's sausages as much as I did and it became a joke for Cliff and his sons, following him in the business, that when we Americans were in the village the consumption of tomato sausages went up a thousand per cent. For we did not do as the village folk did, having just one or two links with potatoes and vegetables; we liked six or seven of them with a little mashed potato to soak up the fat that bubbled out of the links. It was a feast I recall in reveries, and my surviving daughter and I have often shared little fantasies where we have Cliffie ship us a couple of pounds air express. Alas, all things change and often for the worse; my cousin Christine tells me that her mother asserted that, with Cliffie's retirement, his sons had completely ruined the sausage. Perhaps they put meat in it.

One reason that those village folk skimped on sausage and mash was that they were saving a lot of room for dessert. Yorkshire people are very big on sweets, both candy and desserts. (I think it no accident that the best English chocolate makers, Cadbury and Rowntree, had their head-quarters in Yorkshire.) Indeed, for some people tea-time is mostly dessert time, with fruit pies, rich cakes, and cupcakes vying for attention. Once again there is need for translation. An American fruit pie has a near inch of apple or other fruit between the crusts; an English pie has but a trace of fruit spread thin between crusts, so little that my wife was never willing to think of it as a fruit pie. As with the Yorkshire meat pies, for those eating fruit pies the crust was the thing. And then on some occasions there was trifle! My stomach turns at the memory of trifle, a dish that graced our Sunday tea table before the war—and sometimes during the war in a leaner form. I was occasionally unable to go to chapel in the evening because my stomach could not cope with the richness of the trifle served me and I suffered all evening long, unable to enjoy my liberation. The trifle I recall so unhappily was a melange of cake, jello, diced fruit, custard, and cream. Ugh! Where its name came from, I have no idea, but it always seemed singularly inappropriate for a dish that loomed so large in my childhood. We had it so frequently because my father, a notorious sweet-tooth, really liked it.

Earlier I mentioned the great Yorkshire chocolate makers, Cadbury and Rowntree, whose products are not distinctively Yorkshire. That claim belongs to the licorice candies made in Castleford and Pontefract (the place of the broken Roman bridge). In the Pontefract area, I have been told, there is an extraordinary depth of soil that is required for licorice to flourish. The root, as bitter tasting an item as I can imagine, was available in shops during my childhood and, in a particularly curious ritual, we made "licorice water" to accompany the hot cross buns we ate on Good Friday. This we did by soaking a piece of licorice root in a jam jar full of water. Left long enough—

for three or four weeks, perhaps—this produced a dark, oily drink some claimed to enjoy. I could never get started on the soaking in time and my "water" was awful. We carried our jars and buns to a wooded place on the edge of the village that was called Mary Panel Hill. Too steep to ride a bike up, that hill was originally called "Mary Pan Hill" after a witch who lived in the woods, at least that was my mother's story. My pals and I always called it Mary Panel and that was enough for us. But the good of licorice came in the distinctive candy that was manufactured from it. "Pontefract Cakes" were black buttons of chewy sweet stuff, unlike anything I have ever had. I like them and I hope to find some in Chicago on an early visit. Then there were "Licorice Allsorts," a great favorite of mine. These were pieces of black licorice stuff, some flat squares, some short rounds, with various candy pieces attached to them. They must be as bad for young teeth as a sugar bath would be, but I think of them fondly.

No account of Yorkshire fare would be complete without a rhapsody on cheese. A full course Yorkshire dinner ends with a cheese plate, a variety of cheeses to be sampled with crackers. There are several varieties of English cheese, all of them, so far as I know, hard. They range in color from a near-orange to white and in flavor from very sharp to gently mild. My favorite—perhaps chauvinism again—is Wensleydale, the Yorkshire cheese named for a valley in which there is no River Wensley; in this one case the Dale is named for a town. But I'll be generous and mention as a worthy competitor Cheshire, the cheese named for an adjacent county to the west. They are alike in being mild and having a subtle flavor. Happily, my daughter and I are able to buy these in Chicago and it has become something of a tradition with us that we lunch on those cheeses and French bread before I leave her on Sunday at the end of my monthly visits. Eating Wensleydale is nearly my only contact with Yorkshire these days. There could be hardly any better.

Chapter 10
Golden Rule Days

My formal schooling began with what in those days was called the babies' class, the equivalent of an American kindergarten of the time, where we tots were taught by Miss Mills, who surely had a first name, though I never heard anybody use it. My mother, who had known her since they were children, always called her Miss Mills, even in her last years. She was, I believe, a few years my mother's senior, so she was probably in her late forties when she was my teacher. In later years my mother liked to tell people that I had insisted to her that Miss Mills knew everything, and doubtless she seemed omniscient to a five-year old. My memories of my year under her care, while vague, are altogether happy, and I have cherished one particular moment in her classroom. We began each day with a prayer—no separation of church and state there—and we children had been instructed to stand with our eyes closed, our palms together. One morning Molly Brook, who was to grow up to become a local beauty queen, said at the end of the prayer, "Please, Miss Mills, Bruce Haywood had his eyes open." "And how do you know that, Molly Brook?" Miss Mills asked. How could you not love Miss Mills?

Recess was called "play-time" and older pupils were sent out, boys and girls separately, into the asphalt-covered playgrounds that were surrounded by brick walls, there to spend the few minutes morning and afternoon. We of the babies' class were shepherded out by Miss Mills at a time apart from the other classes, doubtless to keep us from observing the rough stuff that went on during play-time, for in the absence of any playground equipment, games of tag and general rough-housing occupied the boys, while the girls skipped rope and stood about chatting. The rule was that the boys and girls, though they sat in classrooms together, remain strictly separated during play-time, which was usually unsupervised. We were particularly instructed to stay well away from the wooden gate that linked the two playgrounds. Only on one occasion, when I was seven or so, did I see boys break the rule and that was when there had been a very unusual snowfall that covered the ground to two or three inches. I was suddenly aware of a group of big boys, seemingly led by my cousin-uncle Jack, piling snowballs by the gate and then, at a signal, opening the gate, crossing into forbidden territo-

ry, and collectively hurling snowballs at screaming girls. The attack can't have lasted more than
a minute or two, but it was the talk of the school
for days after. My memory insists that the mis-
creants were never identified and I knew enough
never to mention Jack's part in it to my mother.
I couldn't resist telling her of the raid, though,
and I got the anticipated frown and "Tut" from
her. I imagine she added, as I know she did on
many an occasion afterward, "I certainly hope
you weren't involved."

Miss Mills lived but a hundred yards from the
school and I often saw her in later years walking
back and forth, a great lady. I always made a point
of crossing to the other side of the street or taking
some other evasive action so that I wouldn't have
to meet her. For I never knew, until I was grown,
how to greet her. How I wish now that I had
written her a note thanking her for putting down
Molly Brook and for all else she did for me.

She was the only one of my teachers who
lived in the village, the others, except the headmaster, coming by bus from Castleford and elsewhere. Teachers in England have traditionally
enjoyed more respect and a better pay-scale than
their American counterparts and the headmaster,
at least until the war, was able to commute by

car. Ownership of a car put him on a par with the village doctor and elevated him considerably in our eyes.

Like Miss Mills, my teachers in the village school were locals who spoke a somewhat refined version of our dialect; I never had any difficulty understanding them. After the babies class there were eight "standards" (grades), numbered one through eight, each with its assigned master or mistress. (I had been in school many years before I learned that "mistress" had another meaning.) Teachers at that level had completed two years at a training college, the kind of place that was called a normal school in this country, and they were likely to serve in the same school all their lives. My mother had raised me to be respectful of teachers and to be intimidated by them; others had evidently received like upbringing, for I never heard a teacher seriously challenged. To be sure, they were given nicknames and were sometimes secretly mocked for their mannerisms, but my fellow pupils respected their authority and even lived in some fear of one of the staff who was quick to use the cane when a pupil misbehaved. Corporal punishment was an accepted feature in those days; it could be a quick slash on the hand with a ruler or a thin cane before the rest of the class, or, in an extreme case, it could be a bad boy being sent to the headmaster's office. There he would be told to pull down his pants and the headmaster would give him five of the best with a thick cane. I remember one or two lads coming back from such an encounter with tears streaming down their faces. I am confident that the knowledge that punishment would be swift and severe was a prime reason for the orderliness of our school rooms.

In those days children were required to stay in school until they were fourteen, but that did not mean that every fourteen-year old completed all eight standards. One year, when I was perhaps eight or nine, I shared a desk with an older boy called Ben Armstrong, then nearly fourteen, who was being kept in the class until he could write his name or, more likely, reach his fourteenth birthday. He was clearly "slow," but he was always friendly and on more than one occasion protected me from bullying by his peers.

The prime emphasis in that school—and a strong and continuing one it was—was on the three Rs. But a strong secondary emphasis was on being English, which meant learning a history of Britain that was a history of kings and queens, of learning patriotic poems and songs, of hearing of the inventions and ideas that English men and women had contributed to the world, and of learning geography in the manner of Aunt Flo, which is to say by seeing those red places on the map that were "ours." In those innocent days it seemed as though the British Empire would defy the rules of history and last forever.

My mother had easily convinced the head-master that I would be a likely winner of a scholarship to the grammar school and that I should appropriately skip a grade or two, so that I would be the better prepared for the competition. Thus, in 1936, the year I was to take the examinations, I was sitting in Standard 7 with children three or four years older than I; I have no sense of having been scarred by that experience. I always found that I could do the work and the older children mostly ignored me. I was smart enough to keep a low profile and answer questions put by the teacher only if they were addressed specifically to me.

And so there came, in the spring of 1936, the Saturday so long anticipated, the day when I would sit for the examinations in English, math, general knowledge, the day that would decide all my future life.

The assumptions and practices of English and American education have been so utterly different over the years as to make useful comparison nearly impossible. I think of young Americans being guided and assisted at every level, always encouraged to seek to ascend to a higher stage, always invited to think of schooling as a pleasant experience, to be enjoyed, even taken lightly. In contrast, I think of the English system as a series of doors along an ever-narrowing corridor, doors through which a shrinking number were permitted to pass, the unhappy rest being left to stay forever at the door that had slammed in their face. Schooling was always proposed to us as the difficult road to a better life, a lonely path to follow, with eager competitors pressing in on us, while stern taskmasters prodded and scolded us along the way—a gloomy, Dickensian image. The last thing we were allowed to expect was any pleasure in learning; always before us, indeed, was the dire consequence of our failing to give our maximum effort, the shame of our not achieving what our parents expected of us. Of course, many children were able early to accept what their marks on exams told them, namely that they were not going to be scholarship material and would therefore have to accept the blue-collar world that awaited them. But even they were pushed and shoved by the system, so that by the time they were fourteen they had achieved a decent level of primary education. Alas, the school system had no place for the "late bloomer" so readily accommodated in the American pattern, but such a one could eventually become a policeman—another respected occupation—go into one of the armed services, or find a niche in the world of business where his aptitudes would be valued. Not everybody, the English system has said implicitly, can or should aspire to academic distinction.

I felt very confident that Saturday morning when I sat down in the examination room, more confident when I left it, for I had had time enough to rewrite my essays and review all my answers to questions on the math and general knowledge papers. I passed, as did three others from my school: two girls, another boy. It was my first step up the ladder my mother had planned that I should climb.

Castleford Grammar School was a world away from my village school and at first I was scared by it and made to feel very inferior for a time. It was, like all English schools of its kind, a pale imitation of England's renowned private schools: Eton, Harrow, Rugby, Winchester. (Exclusive as they are, those schools are confusingly called "public schools" because when they were first created they were alternative to private tutoring.) Yet CGS was at once crucially different from its famous models in that it was not a boarding school. Its pupils were drawn from Castleford and villages surrounding it, nearly 500 boys and girls in all, distributed over six "forms." Until clothing was rationed during the war, the boys were required to wear school blazers—green with gold piping—white shirts, and ties with green and gold stripes—the school colors—while the girls were made to wear white blouses, dark green tunics with a gold sash about the waist, and full-length black stockings. Make-up was taboo, as was any jewelry. Boys and girls alike were required to take off their outdoor shoes and to wear rubber-soled canvas shoes indoors, this sensibly to keep the noise level down. Boys and girls were together in classes, on either side of the room, each side seated in alphabetical order, but there were separate gates at the street for the two sexes and a strict taboo on any encounters inside or outside the school grounds.

My school had a Latin motto—"Possum si volo"—which could be translated as "I can if I want," but was intended to mean "I can succeed if I really want to." CGS called its alumni "Old Legiolians," the name supposedly coming from the Roman name for Castleford, but they were familiarly called Old Legs. (Some of them had gone on to great distinction and their names were mentioned reverently on Prize Day and at the Opening and Closing of the school year.)

In our first month we were selected for membership in one of four "houses," not dormitories in the Eton manner, but organizations for team sports and academic competition, the houses being ranked at year's end on points earned in sports and for class rankings. The boys houses, named for famous sons of Yorkshire, were Alcuin, Cook, Frobisher, Scott, their colors respectively white, blue, red, yellow. (I had so little to do with the girls' side of the school that I cannot remember the name of a single girls' house.) Each house had a captain elected by its members and one of my proudest boasts is that I captained Scott House for two years.

The Latin motto, the "Old Legs," the "houses," the uniforms, all suggest a snobbishness that certainly was a not unimportant aspect of the system. In his addresses to us, J. L. Hampson, M.A., our headmaster, let us know that we were an elite of whom much was expected. He also let us know that our admission to his school had put us on a path to service and to privilege, but one from which we could fall, if we were guilty of any transgression. The consequence of such a fall was always before us: the end of any hope for a career. It was a fear that made us boys understand that to show any interest in girls would be disastrous; I recognize now just how carefully the girls' uniforms had been designed to make them unattractive and sexless.

Our every school day began with an assembly in the Great Hall, where we were ranked by our form, girls in one row, boys in a row behind them, and our teachers along the side. We heard a piece of recorded classical music (my first encounter with it), with Mr. Hampson entering from his office at its end. A senior boy read a passage from the Bible, we sang a hymn from the Anglican hymn book, and Mr Hampson made his announcements. It was all very identity building.

My school made no bones about people being graded and ranked. Every form except the Lower and Upper Sixth had at least two "tracks," the better pupils being put in A, the lesser in B or C. I began in I-A and stayed in A forms through the fifth. In my first year I was kept off balance by the drastic change in school styles and by rubbing shoulders with boys from the middle class—sons of bankers, physicians, dentists *et al*, some of whom were fee payers, not scholarship boys. In consequence I performed well below my mother's expectations and was ranked ninth in the class. This brought on a serious talk with my mother. Thereafter I placed second to Marjorie Lumb (an industrious, focused girl who looked startlingly like my mother), except for one glorious semester in the fifth form when I ranked top (to cheers from the other boys in the class).

One thing to which I had immediately to adjust was the standard English spoken by my teachers, all of whom were university graduates and specialists in subject matters. Now I had English from one teacher, history from another, and so on. My teachers, male and female alike, wore short black gowns, emblems of their being university graduates; they seemed to us to move on an exalted plane. One of the males was famous for his practice of using the edge of his gown to erase things from the blackboard. Some of them, I'm certain, were Yorkshire born, but others were not, and for the first time I had to hear accents that were not ours, a different vocabulary that had to be learned, another idiom. And we were not allowed to respond in our dialect; with our Yorkshire accent, yes, but no longer could we get away with what had passed in the village school. So I quickly found myself living in two linguistic worlds, increasingly comfortable with standard English in the classroom, while I used the dialect with my school friends and in the village. My mother continued to do all she could to get me to avoid using the dialect altogether.

It was in my first year that I began with the subject that became my passion. Every pupil had to take French, then still the language of diplomacy, still the preferred language of cultivated Europeans. I was quickly the best in the class and I was to have excellent teachers for the seven years that I worked at the language, with the headmaster himself teaching the very small class (three of us) in Upper Sixth French. In my second year we had to choose between German and Latin. I opted for German—a decision that probably saved my life—partly because I thought it would be more useful to have German, partly because I did not like the reputation of the Latin master, Patrick Delaney, a man allegedly often seen drunk at the local golf club. Aunt Ella, who knew him socially, warned me against having him as a teacher, but eventually, when I was urged to think of going on to university after the war and would need Latin for admission, I took five years of Latin in one. Delaney, I quickly found, was a first-rate teacher and an altogether amiable man in the classroom. French and German, together with English and history, formed the core of my classes and I excelled in all of them. Unfortunately the fine teacher I began German with was called into the military and his replacement, a sour Welshman, was off-putting, so I did not make the same progress in German that I was making in French. By the time I was seventeen I was the apple of Mr. Hampson's eye and he thought me a sure Distinction winner in the Higher School Certificate examinations in my final year. More importantly, he encouraged me to follow in his footsteps and to seek to serve in the Intelligence Corps when I should join the army. By 1943, my final school year, the government had ceased to grant a year's deferment to boys who wanted to study the humanities in university, though potential scientists were still being deferred. Mr. Hampson called me to his office—causing me some moments of near panic—to explain that, if I were to volunteer at the end of the academic year, rather than wait to be drafted, I could choose my army branch. With my knowledge of French and German I would be a sure bet for the Intelligence Corps. Only after my six weeks of primary training was I told that the army was not taking anybody under twenty-one into Intelligence. But by the time my infantry training was nearing its end in early 1944, the need for German speakers had so escalated that the age limit was lowered and I was able to transfer. Thus did taking German likely save my life, for the West Yorkshire infantry platoon I had trained with suffered 90% casualties on D–Day.

Of course, I was not allowed to limit my studies to those four favorite subjects. For the School Certificate Examination in my fifth year—public examinations written in my school under very strict supervision and graded by external examiners—I "sat" for nine subjects: English Language, English Literature, French, German, History, Biology, Art, Mathematics, Geography. Along the way I had brief encounters with Chemistry and Physics (not my cup of tea), as well as Religious Studies in my first year, and, also in my first year, Woodworking. That last was my worst experience in all my schooling. The British Army, testing me in my first weeks of training, certified that I had no mechanical aptitude, something poor Mr. Ingham could have told them emphatically. He did his best to show me how to use a saw, a chisel, a plane, but I proved unable to master them. Eventually, throwing up his hands in despair, he put me to work repairing broken chairs. Meanwhile my classmates were happily producing bookends, candlesticks, and other ornaments for their proud parents, items that were suitably sanded, stained, and varnished. How I used to wish I could have made just one object that could have been called my work. Still, there were lots of chairs that needed legs glued to seats, backs glued back in place, and in the end CGS was better served by my repair efforts than my parents would have been by book ends.

Throughout my school years I had gym and sports. Perhaps the most obvious and radical difference between my school and its American counterpart was the absence from my school of any person who could remotely be called a coach. There was a gym master for the boys, "Cod" Atherton, a sweet man who put us through an hour of exercises and games that were designed to make healthy bodies. We had gym just once a week and the pace of it was such that I never worked up a sweat. When I lift weights now, as I occasionally do, I think of Mr. Atherton and follow some of the routines he put us through, but with five-pound weights I work up a sweat.

Besides soccer, cricket, and rugby (the one sport I excelled in and even played in the army), I played "fives," a form of handball played in a peculiar court which was said to be copied from a ruined monastery where the game had been invented. In none of these sports was I ever coached by an adult; older boys offered instruction and team captains advice. We were taught to think about sports in the Eton way: "It isn't whether you win or lose; it's how you play the game." The behavior of English soccer fans these days tells me that that motto has long since been forgotten.

I liked running and I was pretty good at it. In my last year I was the best in the school in the 440 (at a pace a highschool girl would sneer at these days), and the best javelin tosser. One of my best moves as captain of Scott House was my organization of our relay team on my last Sports Day. We were not given much of a chance against rival Alcuin, which had the school's two fastest hundred-yard sprinters, but I carefully evaluated which of us could have the best

chance against the four they were fielding. They
had decided to put their two sprinters in second
and third position, where they would have to
run 220 laps, starting with a boy who was not as
fast as our boy Milner, third fastest in the school
over the hundred yards. I calculated that Milner
would pass the baton to Stenner with a lead of
a few yards, that though Stenner and Oates
would lose ground to the Alcuins I might hope
to get the baton with the final Alcuin runner no
more than a yard or two ahead of me. In fact, my
three fellows ran so well that I got the baton on
a level with Alcuin' best 440 man and I held him
off at the first turn and finished several yards
ahead of him. I have never had a more delicious
triumph in my life. But Sports Day was a down-
er for me at the same time, for I placed only
third in the javelin throw, an event that was mine
to take. I had over-trained and my good right
arm failed me.

The fifth form was the time of another
weeding-out. Only a small number stayed on
to take university-entrance courses in the
Lower and Upper Sixth, the rest "leaving" (we
never said graduating), and going into appren-
ticeships in white-collar professions like
accounting, finding employment in their

fathers' businesses, or becoming clerks of one sort or another. My parents, resolving that somehow they would find the money for me to have three years of university rather than two at a teachers college, helped me to pass through another crucial door.

American schools are quick to spot unusual talent in athletes and to encourage their specialization in sports. The English have long done that in academics subjects. I was allowed to divorce myself at sixteen from mathematics and the sciences and enter Sixth Form Arts, even as others of my classmates opted for Sixth Form Science. At that exalted level we became premature specialists, narrowing our focus to just four subjects, including the couple we would take in university. Thus did I spend my last two years of school on English, French, German, History, the four that had long been my delight and my strength. Marjorie Lumb, I can happily report, opted for Science and I was left a clear path to the Form Prize. Just a couple of years ago, severely pruning my collection of books, I gave away the biography of Goethe I had chosen as my award; some premonition must have told me that the greatest of Germans was going to be at the center of my professional life.

There was one form of gender discrimination that my school practiced, namely treating boys and girls differently on rainy days. In the lunch hour on such days the girls were allowed to dance to phonograph records in the Great Hall. The boys were not allowed back into the building if the rain were light; if it poured we were allowed to go to our classrooms and sit quietly. Either as a form of protest against this discriminatory treatment or just as a prank, some of us sixth-formers one day decided to disrupt the dancing. The hall was two stories high, with windows that pierced its interior wall at the upper level. They could be opened from the second story corridor that ran the full length of the hall. Half a dozen of us, guided by a budding scientist in our number, took long glass tubes from the physics lab. I have no idea what their purpose was in the laboratory, but our leader had recognized the potential of the one end that had the shape of a trumpet's mouthpiece. We stuck those long tubes through the opened windows, attracting no attention from down below until we put our lips to the mouthpiece and blew a Gabriel's blast. The noise was shattering. The girls below screamed satisfyingly and stopped their twirling, but we bolted from the scene of our triumph when the door to Mr. Hampson's office was flung open and the headmaster charged out like a bull into the arena. We had calculated that he would run to the flight of stairs at the end of the building closer to his office, so we made our escape by the stairs at the other end. Surprisingly, we were never questioned and there was never a consequence, other than the delicious sense we conspirators carried with us for the rest of the school year. It is a lasting, childishly fond memory of my final year in school.

I loved Castleford Grammar School. My seven years there were a continuing joy to me. I had good friends, I was a star pupil, my teachers were nearly uniformly interesting and good, I rarely got into trouble and then usually only for responding to a whisper from Gilbert Harvey, who sat in front of me for five years and whose back-of-head I can see to this day. I was wonderfully happy and I choked when, at our last assembly, we sang the traditional end-of-year hymn, "Lord, dismiss us with Thy blessing." I have never had occasion to sing that hymn since.

Before I went into the army I had been granted admission to the honors program at the University of Leeds for some future year, should I survive the war. I had been admitted as one who sought to become a prep school teacher of French and German, the English system of that time requiring that a candidate for university entrance be committed to a career track. Students went directly to the study of medicine or law; there was no preparatory undergraduate education for those professions, as there is here. The university was to prepare students to serve the country's needs for professionals; I never heard anybody suggest that education would afford us a liberalizing experience, other than one that might emerge from our professional studies.

That little had changed in English assumptions by the nineteen-sixties was brought home to me in a conversation I had with an Oxford don who was visiting this country. By then I was the Provost of Kenyon College. He had come to Kenyon because a schoolmate of his was a professor there. The latter, relatively new to this country after years of teaching in Lebanon, was unable to answer the don's questions about American practices and so brought him to my office. Our visitor was perplexed by many of the things he had seen and heard in our little liberal arts college, but he was, at the same time, happily impressed by much else. Along the way he had learned that among our seven hundred students were a dozen Classics majors. Would there be, he asked perplexed, so large a demand for secondary school teachers of Latin that these people would find jobs when they graduated? Recognizing a misunderstanding that once was mine, I explained the basic assumption of the liberal arts college: that study in the liberal arts would provide our students enriched personal lives even as they equipped themselves with the tools for professional study in graduate and professional schools. I happened to know, I said, that not a one of the senior Classics majors contemplated a teaching career; two of them had already been admitted to medical school, some others were heading for law school. He shook his head, astonished. "We could never allow that, of course," he said solemnly. Thank God that America can and does.

Form 5 Alpha of Castleford Grammar School. Being "form captain" (elected by my classmates), I am seated to the left of the "form master," Mr. Delaney, who taught Latin. All the girls are in the school uniform, but by this time (1940) rationing had caused my school to exempt the boys from the requirement. My nemesis, Marjorie Lumb, is seated to the left of me, while the only other Allerton Bywater child, Molly Crossland, is the girl seated in front of Delaney. I was fifteen when this photograph was taken, while most in the class were already sixteen.

Chapter 11
Distractions

It was a very happy thing for me that my two children were daughters. I was sure I would fail as a father of sons, for, not having grown up in this country, I would not have known how to pass on to boys the lore and skills that an American-born father would have acquired in his growing up: shooting baskets, pitching a baseball, saying whatever it is that a quarterback says to a center when he is ready to take the football. Not that I would have fared all that much better, had I fathered sons in England. For I was not an all-round athlete, not a born player. In rugby I eventually found a team sport where I could do more than hold my own, and I was happy about that, for I had not been able to impress my friends before then with my accomplishments. Still, I had at least attempted the things my pals did.

Little boys in Allerton were expected to pass two tests on their way to being admitted to big-boyhood, the one the "long drop," the other the "long crawl." The second was by far the less demanding of the two, provided that one was not afraid of dark tunnels and skinned knees. It required only that a boy crawl on hands and knees the full length of a drain that ran beneath the railroad embankment to the north of the recreation ground. It was a narrow pipe, perhaps twenty-four inches in diameter, with a thin trickle of water running through it. There were probably times after heavy rains when that trickle was a flood, but I was never close to the drain at such a time. Before I ever attempted the crawl I peered through the pipe, in the company of a pal or two, to see whether there really was light at the end of the tunnel. There was, but it seemed faint and terribly distant. I was not eager to try to get to it, but eventually either the Haywood family honor or pressure from big lads caused me to summon up the blood, stiffen the upper lip, and get on my hands and knees. The worst part about it, I still remember vividly, was the awful smell of the water trickling just below my nose. That guaranteed that, once through the tunnel, I never wanted to try it again.

In marked contrast, once I had accomplished the long drop, I did it over and over again. But I shrank from the first attempt for a long time.

Close to the river was a concrete wall—what remained of a site where coal wagons had once been tipped into waiting barges. It was eight or nine feet high, about twice my height when I first attempted the drop. The drill was that a boy lower himself until he was clinging with his finger tips to the edge of the wall, his toes up against the concrete. Then, let go! Gravity took care of the rest. The rest, I was easily able to understand by watching older boys attempting the drop, might include a badly sprained ankle, skinned knees (English boys of my generation wore short pants till they started shaving), a busted nose, or even a nasty bump on the back of the head, if the boy lost his balance on landing and fell backwards. To say nothing of damaged hands and wrists. I, without a trace of masochism in my make-up, watched with mounting dismay and not a little fear. The more athletic types brought off the drop gracefully and without damage to themselves, but I did not count myself among their number. I could only guess at the likely form of my particular injury. But once again something prevailed over my doubts and anxiety. I angled my body over the edge, held on with finger tips for a brief moment, and dropped. I did it perfectly and exuberance rose within me like a volcano's lava. After that I thought myself an acrobat and would go over the edge at the drop of a hat. Until one day I missed my landing and went over backwards. I think I may still have the bump on the back of my head. End of pride.

In truth I did both these "dares" when I was six or seven—and without my mother's knowledge—because I wanted the approval of my friends. For the same reason I tried my best to play both of England's national games, cricket and soccer. Each demands a very particular quality, if you want to be a player. To be any good at soccer, you must be able to kick with both feet; I had enough trouble kicking effectively with the one foot. Cricket demands, besides the obvious need for coordination of hand and eye, athleticism and quickness, that a batsman be infinitely patient. Whereas in baseball a batter must run if he hits the ball fair, a cricketer may hit successive balls all afternoon without running. He can bide his time and wait for just the right ball to come along—and wait and wait. He runs only when he is sure he can get to the other end of the pitch and score a run. Patience is not among my virtues and I always attempted to hit balls that were not to be hit. I never made the first team. It will be obvious that watching cricket being played demands patience nearly equal to that displayed by the batter; games may last all day—or two or three days—with appropriate breaks for lunch and tea.

One of the unhappy signs of England's decline as a world power is that other countries routinely defeat England's teams in the two sports England has given the world. Australia, India, Jamaica, former "possessions," now produce cricketers who outplay England's in "test matches," as the international competitions are called. It is even worse in soccer. That game, an English philosopher has recently said, will survive when all other of England's gifts to the world have disappeared, but it seems likely that it will not be played at the highest level in England. It is the international sport above all others and by now teams from South America, Africa, Asia, and Europe regularly trounce England's. England, to be sure, is still producing some outstanding players, but there is unmistakable evidence of what has befallen England in the fact that at least one major league English team in 2006 had not one player on it who had been born English.

Only in my third year at Castleford Grammar School did I discover rugby. By then I was big enough to look like somebody who could stand being knocked about a bit and so the big lads invited me in on lunch-time pick-up games. I had learned enough by watching from the sideline that I was able to be a participant and I quickly found out on the field that my quickness and my good hands would be enough to make me a player. I improved by learning from older and better players. I quickly understood both team play and what was expected of me. Rugby is a player's sport, not a spectator's, a game that has a team playing offense one minute, defense a second later. In my day there was no substitution; an injured player meant playing a man short. Rugby can seem from the sidelines like an endless confusion, and even a player may find himself wondering where on earth the ball went to. But it was the game I came to love and I can still feel the pleasure of trotting out on the field, cleats biting into the turf, and the rush of adrenaline that accompanied the kick-off. I loved the game so much that I played it on a Saturday afternoon after doing a week of tough infantry training, on a team captained by a wonderfully gifted player who had led England's international team before the war. He had a gentle name, Hubert Lockwood, but he had been tough enough to play with the best. I gave up rugby when I went to intelligence school, but I would very likely have taken it up again, if I had stayed in England.

At the end of my year in the Lower Sixth, our headmaster wrote on my annual report that I "seemed not to understand the implications of sixth form work." He was warning my parents and me that, if I did not do the work I was capable of doing, I might not get to university. My mother didn't understand his "implications," though she knew there was a warning of some sort there, even though my marks ranked me first in the class. Mr. Hampson was right; I should and could have been working harder at my studies. I was doing just enough to keep me on the honor roll, but I could have been doing distinguished work, had I really given my full attention to my subjects.

It wasn't rugby that was distracting me and it wasn't girls. It was the piano.

Among the most stupid things I ever did was to reject the offer of a helpful German inform- ant when I was stationed in Bremerhaven in 1945. Learning that I played the piano, he offered to put me in touch with a renowned pianist in the community, he obviously believing that I would value the opportunity to study with a cel- ebrated teacher. Why did I not seize it? Was it that, with the war barely over, I could not accept the idea of subordinating myself to a German? It may have been that I was enjoying my freedom from the teachers who had hovered over me all my life to that point. In any event I didn't follow up on his offer. Had I accepted it, I should have been a disciplined student of the piano for the first time.

I began when I was eight, with my father as teacher. I remember a lot of tears from me and impatient noises from my Dad. Barely able himself to play even a simple hymn correctly, he was in no position to teach even a willing pupil, and I'm certain I was not that. But it was a way of getting me started without having to pay a teacher. After a few months he decided to apprentice me to his oldest brother, Robert, our chapel organist. I was with Uncle Robert for two years, months of slow progress through the easier pieces of minor composers, whose works I came to know in dog-eared albums bought at second-hand bookstores. They were tuneless at a time when I needed melody. But practice made me dextrous, to the point that Uncle Robert, his own fingers growing stiff with age and work in the pit, recommended that my father find me a younger and more able teacher.

It was, in fact, my mother who "asked around" and settled on Mrs. Bickerdike and it was with

Mrs. Bickerdike that I blossomed. She understood my need for melodies that would engage my ear and make me wish to master them. She moved me quickly to more demanding pieces and insisted that I practice them carefully. But she was too indulgent and let me get away without practicing scales and arpeggios, as a sterner teacher would not have done. I have never made up that neglect, but I continue to be grateful that Mrs. Bickerdike let me find joy in playing.

By the time I was fourteen Mrs. Bickerdike thought me good enough to take her place in the small dance band she played in on Friday and Saturday evenings and she told me to ask my parents for permission to sit beside her for a few evenings until I should have understood what would be expected of me. This precipitated a small crisis. I was very eager to become a dance band pianist, for I had come to be a fan of the big bands that were swinging the music of Hoagy Carmichael, Cole Porter, and the like. I was eagerly listening to the radio and learning names like Artie Shaw, Glenn Miller, Duke Ellington; my romance with American jazz was beginning. My parents were not pleased with this and made the kind of derogatory remarks about my "kind of music" that I make about today's rockers. It was a long way from Methodist hymns. And then there was the Catholic part.

My mother had swallowed a good piece of her anti-Catholic feelings in deciding on Mrs Bickerdike, for my teacher-to-be was a practicing Catholic. But now the issue became the fact that those Friday and Saturday dances were held at the Catholic church hall in Castleford and on behalf of the Catholic church. Moreover, all the members of the little band—six in all—were Catholic! There was no end to it. My parents debated, questioned, objected. I cited my approved friendship with Frank Kelly that had brought me no closer to sin. I even offered the fact that, my apprenticeship over, I would be paid for playing! Perhaps it was that good Yorkshire instinct for the-penny-earned that carried the day. I was given permission, if not approval.

Soon Mrs. Bickerdike left the bench to me and I took to fox-trots, waltzes, tangos, like a duck to water, memorizing pieces quickly so that I was able to watch the dancers even while I played. But with time I came to envy the musicians who played melody instruments—trumpet, trombone, sax—while I played in the "rhythm section," vamping as we used to say, behind the leaders. So after a couple of years I began to dream of playing alto saxophone and, in the summer after I had successfully passed the School Certificate Examination and been admitted to the Sixth Form, I persuaded my parents to lend me the money to buy one. I taught myself, using a "guide to the saxophone" I found on a market stall, and before long I was up front with the melody makers and a woman had taken my place at the piano. I gave up the sax, as I did rugby, when I went to intelligence school, but my mother held on to my instrument for several years, always hoping, evidently, that it might be among the things that would attract me back to England. I had parted from it with no regrets, knowing that I would never be a Charlie Parker.

Bad enough, in terms of my commitment to my studies, that I should be spending Friday and Saturday nights in this dubious activity. But our reputation grew—a little—and we were invited to Wednesday night and Saturday afternoon gigs in other-than-Catholic venues. I was paying off the loan on my sax far more quickly than I had imagined I would.

What Mr. Hampson somehow recognized— he must have had a very efficient grapevine that kept him abreast of his pupils' activities—was that music had come to occupy first place in my life and a kind of music, moreover, which he would not consider appropriate to a future university student and teacher. His message on my end-of-year report was intended to give me gentle warning, and warn me it did. I was more attentive to my work in the Upper Sixth than I had been in the previous year, so that even while I continued to be intensely occupied with music, I was able to please Mr. Hampson with my classroom performance. Yet I can acknowledge that I could have and should have done better. The story of my life....

Chapter 12
Blackout

On the first Sunday in September, 1939 Adolf Hitler, not appeased by the concessions Britain and France had made him, sent his tanks into Poland. A solemn BBC announcer told us before many hours had gone by that the Allies, honoring their commitments to Poland, had declared war on Germany. World War II had officially begun. My mother gave a deep sigh and said, "Well, at least Bruce won't have to go." It was about three weeks before my fourteenth birthday.

Like many people in England, my mother thought the war would be over in a very few weeks, for she and they were certain that England had secret weapons that would quickly defeat the Germans.

We had been on a seaside vacation in the last week of August, staying at a boarding house run by my Aunt Sadie, with an assist from my mother's brother Tom, and the talk in the dining room there had been all of war and the prospect of war. The room was about equally divided between those who, with my father, scoffed at the very idea that there might be a war—"The Gerries would never dare start another, not after the way we beat 'em last time"—and those who, while believing that war would come, confidently expected that those secret weapons would immediately be unleashed and that the war would be over by Christmas.

The story I heard most frequently in those days was about a man who was driving his car along a coastal road, when his engine suddenly quit. Puzzled, he got out of his car and lifted the hood, but before he could look for a loose wire a man appeared from behind the bushes and told him that his engine would start again in a moment or two. "I can't tell you just what is going on here, sir, " he said, " but I can tell you that you are on the edge of a government test area." That "death ray," as one story-teller after another called it, was going to cause German tanks to stop in their tracks and German planes to fall out of the sky. We would achieve victory before there was any need to send our troops into action! And even if there were no secret weapons, we could beat the Germans; we'd done it before. The English had obviously not been listening to Winston Churchill's warnings about Hitler's build-up of army, navy, and air force; they would pay bitterly for those years between the wars when pacifism and head-in-the-sand politics dominated English life.

The nose has its memory and mine can still recapture the fetid gas mask I was issued some weeks after the war got under way. I carried my mask everywhere in its cardboard box; we were required to have it with us at all times. We had regular drills when we pulled the awful thing over our face and breathed through the filter, pretending that the Germans had dropped gas bombs about us. Soon after the gas mask, every family living in a house was presented with a stack of metal forms and a bag of bolts that could be assembled into a small air-raid shelter.

The Anderson shelter wasn't designed to withstand a hit from a bomb; it was intended to grant protection from bricks and other debris that might fall from a nearby bombed building. My father enlisted my help in digging out a hole behind our house, a couple of feet deep. I remember we got down to clay. Then, carefully following the written instructions, we bolted the several pieces of metal together to form what looked something like a tiny Quonset hut. We stacked sandbags about it. There was no floor other than the tromped earth, but we put down a piece of tar paper. Not a place to spend happy hours, but into it we went on the first several occasions when the sirens warned us that bombers were approaching. The Germans followed Yorkshire rivers to their targets, the munition factories in the Leeds area, and we would hear their engines drone and even catch a glimpse of a plane caught by a searchlight's probing beam. Later we would see the flashes of exploding bombs, followed in seconds by a loud thump. On only one occasion did bombs fall at all close to our village, but Castleford, at the junction of two rivers, had houses and other buildings hit on several occasions, presumably by bombs that were mistakenly dropped there.

Archie Parker, a near neighbor who had three fully grown sons, set to work to build a shelter that was to be a palace compared to the Anderson. It was large enough for the five Parkers and guests as well, and we were soon invited to join the Parkers there. With concrete walls, floor and roof, well away from the Parker's house, it featured hurricane lamps and a paraffin stove for cold nights. I remember benches, lawn chairs, and thermoses of hot tea, as well as a lot of cheerfully defiant banter. I sometimes joined my father and Archie on their occasional trips up the steps to watch the distant flashes.

But such pleasures at two or three in the morning quickly palled and my father and I soon resolved that we were going to stay in our beds during the raids, convinced as we were that the Germans would never mistake Allerton for a munitions factory. But my mother had no such confidence in the enemy and she continued to pull on clothes over her nightgown and walk over to the Parkers. After a time the Germans gave up on the north of England and concentrated their bombers on London in what became famous as "the Blitz." The Parkers quickly converted their shelter into a storage cellar for pig food and straw; one of their contributions to the war effort was to breed and raise hogs.

Everybody was called on to contribute in one way or another. Every Briton between eighteen and forty, male and female alike, had to perform some kind of war work. For the majority, of course, that meant service in one of the armed forces or, for some young women, in the Land Army, where they drove farm tractors, milked cows, sheared sheep, and even killed rats. On one memorable day I watched a pair of Land Army girls prepare a large barn for ratting by sealing most of the holes and stationing fox terriers by the two exits they left open. Then they put a pair of ferrets into a hole and, cudgels in hand, waited with the enthusiastic, similarly armed farm hands for the panic-stricken rats to bolt. I see again those unbelievably quick little dogs, snapping at necks, dropping their dead victims, the Land Army girls and the farm hands hitting and slashing at the rats that tried to escape by running up vertical walls. It was a few minutes of exultant slaughter before the ferrets emerged and were packed away for another day. They would be back in a year's time, when the rats would have re-colonized and produced their several hundred offspring.

Before I went into the army I made my little contributions to the war effort, as a fire-watcher and by working in my school's harvest camps.

There were fire-watchers everywhere, which is to say people who stayed up all night on the alert for the incendiary bombs that became a standard German weapon against our cities. My school needed protection and members of the Sixth Form, Upper and Lower, were invited to serve. There were girls' teams as well as boys', with five members, and we worked a full night every couple of weeks. "Worked" meant that we spent an evening doing our homework, with a fish'n'chip supper fetched by one of the group about nine or ten o'clock, followed by a night of sleep on cots. (That very small room had windows that opened, I can happily report.) There was a master—or a mistress for the girls—on duty throughout, as much to chaperon us as to lead the charge if a bomb fell. We were given instruction in how to cope with an incendiary bomb, which was to cover it immediately with a fine spray so that it would quickly burn itself out. Fortunately we never had to test our skills. I remember many happy nights with friends and some evenings when I would go down into the main hall and play the school's grand piano in total darkness. In those days I had a lot of music committed to memory.

Far more of a contribution came through the late summer weeks I spent harvesting potatoes. A group of us—some two dozen senior boys and three or four masters and their wives—traveled by bus to the flat lands of the county to the south of us, Lincolnshire. We went specifically to the little village of Crowland, a place renowned for its ruined abbey and a peculiar three-cornered bridge that crossed a no-longer-existing stream. There we were housed in the village school, to sleep on straw mattresses on the floor, to eat breakfasts and suppers prepared by our teachers' wives, and to go out thence to nearby farms. The land, we were told, had been claimed from the North Sea a century before and now the rich soil yielded potatoes in abundance. I was assigned with a half-dozen of my fellows to the Drury's farm, a place of ancient buildings and but one small tractor. That, the only thing on the farm with an engine, pulled along a device called a spinner, which neatly cut through the rows and threw the potatoes out on the ground before us pickers. We crawled along on our hands and knees, picking up the harvest and putting the spuds into small baskets that, once filled, were tipped into a "trug," a large wickerwork basket that stood at the end of the row. After a couple of days I, being the tallest, took the place of one of the farmer's sons as tipper and I built muscle hoisting those weighty baskets and tipping the potatoes into a two-wheeled cart. Two carts were needed to keep things moving and they were drawn by magnificent horses, Percherons, the pride of George, the youngest of the farmer's four sons, who in the off season showed them at county fairs and even at the big agricultural shows in London. Those horses knew their way around the farm, always gauging their turns to get through gateways and narrow passages by the farm buildings. I became very fond of them, until one of them put his giant foot on mine, pressing it down into the soft earth. Had I been standing on cement, I should have had broken bones.

We had a couple of happy weeks on the farm, eating boiled potatoes in their jackets as an accompaniment to our lunch-time sandwiches and being given glasses of rich milk from the Drury's only cow. Once we were given a very special treat, when we were invited to eat dinner with the family. We were served a ragout of pheasant, hare, and rabbit, those creatures having been the victims of the tractor-driver son, who always had a shotgun with him. From time to time as we worked we would hear a shot and a cry of triumph.

Of an evening we flirted with London girls who had been evacuated to the village to escape the bombing, they laughing at our accents as much as we marveled at theirs. On Saturday we were allowed to take the bus into Peterborough to see a movie. It was in Peterborough that I saw my first American, a black GI, who was wearing a uniform that, by British standards, seemed downright gaudy, so be-medalled and be-ribboned was the soldier. We were surprised to find him walking alone on a city street. I have since wondered whether he survived D-Day.

Those extra potatoes for lunch and that wonderful dinner were very welcome, for in the wartime years of my adolescence I was always hungry. Indeed, I stayed hungry in my army years too, until my good fortune took me to work with American intelligence in Germany at the war's end. Food rationing in England began in the first weeks of the war and grew more and more severe. Our government assured us, nearly every day it seemed, that we were all being treated fairly and alike, but this was obviously never the case. Those who could afford to eat in restaurants could get extra food that way, while those with land, even acreage as small as ours and the Parkers', could always supplement their rations with eggs and vegetables. Our small island country was dependent on the importation of foodstuffs and the German U-boats did their best to cut off our supplies. But cans of Spam got through and that processed meat became a lifesaver, fried, broiled, eaten cold. Yes, comedians made awful jokes about it, but I remember it gratefully. People who had no chickens got one egg a week (later one a month!), and if that egg were bad... tough. Meat was particularly scarce and housewives became ingenious at preparing meat meals without meat. Yorkshire pudding came into its own.

I have heard many people say, reflecting on the war years, that the hardest thing to endure was the blackout. The public was quickly informed after the war began that enemy bombers would be helped to their targets, if any lights were visible below them. Strict regulations were imposed and wardens were hired to patrol districts to check for violations. For us the black-out meant first the job of installing heavy curtains on every window and trips outside to check for any leaks. All street-lighting was shut down; operators of vehicles were required to cover headlights nearly completely, with only a small slit left; shops and stores covered windows and doors; lights had to be turned off when somebody entered a building so that no light would filter through an open door. With flash-lights outlawed, we learned to grope our way along the darkened streets, sometimes bumping painfully into lampposts or coming into jarring contact with a fence. Moonlight nights were greeted enthusiastically. "Put that light out" became a national slogan. People getting off a bus would hope to find a neighbor walking their way. For my father and other bus drivers the blackout was torment.

For a few people the blackout was a new opportunity. Robberies were on the increase, there were reports of women being molested. And there was the Halifax slasher.

Halifax is a Yorkshire industrial town some twenty miles from Allerton. There, in the third year of the war, a woman reported to the police that a man had slashed her face as she walked home alone in the late evening from her munitions factory job. Our newspaper showed a picture of what looked like a razor cut on the woman's cheek. Within a short span of time there was a second report, another photograph, and soon there was a report every other day or so. A reporter dubbed the anonymous attacker "the Halifax slasher" and women feared to go out alone, lest they become the slasher's victims.

The scare lasted several weeks, but eventually the police reported that it was all a hoax. The first woman had confessed that she inflicted the cut upon herself and others soon made the same admission.

What prompted those women to do it? Were they so eager to have a photograph in the paper? So eager to have their name known? I think it was a response to a life that seemed hemmed in, restricted on every side, dull, monotonous, blacked out. Those women, their husbands and boyfriends gone to war, were lonely and depressed. There was no outlet for their frustration until the first woman, in a frenzied moment, cut her cheek and invented the excitement of a faceless attacker.

A few years ago I saw an English movie called "Land of Hope and Glory" that chronicled the first couple of years of the war, seen through the eyes of a small boy, as one working class family experienced it. The writer of the film and I were born in the same year; his memories were like mine. What I found altogether compelling about the film was that it showed what happened essentially on the one street where the family lived, with the great movements and events between 1939 and 1941 at a far distance, referred to only in passing. But the realities were a strayed barrage balloon, a bombed house a block away, rationing, hand-me-down clothing, a soldier home on a brief leave, lovers separated, and the blackout. That was the way we children, we civilians, really experienced the war. It was all very, very dull.

Parents were usually unable to understand why their sons and daughters, with the war

seemingly stalemated in its middle years, welcomed the call to the armed forces. They wanted to put it down to patriotism and the will to
serve. I'm convinced, having listened to so many
of my school friends and fellow soldiers, that it
was the opportunity to break out of the stifling
boredom that made people eager to serve, as
much as any sense of doing one's duty. Change
meant that something different was happening,
that just maybe the course of the war would
alter. But in 1943, when I enlisted, at least two of
my teachers thought the war might last a hundred years, simply extending until every country
involved was exhausted and a settlement was
reached, for it was impossible for them—and
many others—to imagine that there could be a
successful invasion of Fortress Europe. We had
given up believing in death rays.

Chapter 13
The Road to America

My mother and my schoolteacher aunts combined to make sure that I spent a goodly part of my childhood reading the masterpieces of children's literature produced by English authors. The English have a special gift for creating enchanting tales that appeal to adults as much as they do to children. J. K. Rowling's Harry Potter novels are the latest gems of the genre and I am certain that, had they appeared in my young days, I would have been like those millions of children and adults around the world who have devoured every word in them. In fact, after reading the first two and satisfying my curiosity about their success, I left Harry and his pals and returned to the magic of my own world.

I am eternally grateful for my immersion in the wonderful stories I read in my childhood and I have gone back to them from time to time, particularly in introducing my own children to them. I was introduced early to Lewis Carroll's Alice and her wondrous adventures and to A. A. Milne's Pooh tales that were still relatively new on the scene, together with his witty and delightful poems. The rhythms of "James

James Morrison Morrison/Weatherby George Dupree" often bounce across my mind today and I cherish images of Christopher Robin and Pooh climbing stairs together or musing on adult follies.

There was a Pooh in my own life. Somebody—I have since forgotten who—gave me a stuffed toy elephant when I was very small. My mother told me his name was Jumbo and that is what he remained. It was many a year before I knew that the name came from P. T. Barnum's monster. What an absurd name that was for my Jumbo, who was a wee thing, his trunk just a few inches long. But he occupied a large place in my bed for many years, the little brother I never had, and he was my companion in my bed-time adventures. When my bed was a submarine, Jumbo was navigator to my captain and guided us towards the German ships we were seeking to attack. When my bed was a plane bombing German trenches, Jumbo was co-pilot and bombardier. He manned the heavy gun on our tank as we crushed German soldiers beneath our treads. He always seemed to know that one day it would be the Germans we would have to fight again. Jumbo was ready for the fray. Indeed, he must have been wounded in action at some point, because I remember my mother having to stitch him up. I don't remember just when I finally gave Jumbo up, though I'm certain it was before I went in the army.

It was not from my children's literature that I got those warlike imaginings. The books were nearly all peaceable, though the villainous otters in my favorite, Kenneth Graham's *The Wind in the Willows*, were a bloodthirsty lot. I was well into my twenties, I think, before I could see otters as the playful creatures they are. I read Graham over and over: Rat rowing his little boat along the river to visit his river-bank friend Mole; the megalomaniac Toad with his painted caravan and opulent motor car; the furry little animals having cups of tea and scones—these are images that persist in my mind and cause me still to smile fondly.

But as I grew a little older those oh-so-English works were replaced in my immediate affection by American novels. I was introduced to them by a teacher in my village school, Miss Dacre, a tiny little thing who nonetheless had a reputation for administering a smart cut with the cane. A favorite poem of hers was Joyce Kilmer's "Trees," though she unwittingly led us children astray on two points. First, she left us believing that the poet was a woman. Like her, we had never heard of a male Joyce; there were two girls in the class named Joyce, a common girl's name in those days Then she asked us what mistake the poet had made in the line "A nest of robins in her hair." A boy in the front row promptly corrected the "mistake," saying that robins build their nests on the ground. He, a notorious stealer of eggs and "ragger" of birds' nests, knew all about English robins and their practices, but neither he nor Miss Dacre knew that Kilmer's American robin was an altogether different breed of bird. It was, of course, named after its distant English relative; in both countries the robin's red breast makes it a favorite. There is a profound truth in the line that Winston Churchill was fond of quoting: "The English and the American are two peoples divided by a common language."

My great debt to little Miss Dacre (who never laid a hand on me, I'm glad to say, given her reputation), is for her having introduced me to Mark Twain. In her class I made the acquaintance of that prototypical American boy, Tom Sawyer, a lad my mother would have frowned on, I know. I took him to my heart and I lived vicariously in his world. I read the novel a dozen times, Becky Thatcher and the others becoming as real to me as Allerton folk, but I never shared my passion with a friend. A little later I met Huck Finn and floated down the great river with him and Jim, often more than a little confused by Twain's idiom, awe struck by the images of the Mississippi he evoked. Today I live less than forty miles from that remarkable stream and just last evening I dined at a restaurant hard by the Mississippi, where we watched a bald eagle float slowly overhead, hunting for fish. I have thought that my life seems to have moved in a sort of circle, returning me at last to a favorite place of my childhood.

An aunt gave me the other American novel of my young years, a present on a birthday, perhaps my tenth. It was *The Last of the Mohicans* and I was entranced by it. Once again I lived in the novel's world, reading its best passages over and over till I had nearly memorized them. This was a very different world from Twain's Missouri river town, a world far more difficult to picture in my imagination, for there was nothing in Yorkshire to compare. We had rivers and towns beside them, but we had no forests. At that point in my life I had not seen even a large wood. James Fenimore Cooper took me into a seemingly infinite wilderness, peopled with danger and violence and yet breathtaking in its beauty and appeal. Again, fate has seemed to bring me back to a childhood world, for I eventually came to Michigan's Upper Peninsula, my wife's home ground and a place that is still like Cooper's America in many respects. There I have stood where the vast forest and Lake Superior greet each other and, as I rested beneath a pine and looked out on the big sea's shining water, I could imagine that I was the first man ever to stand in that lonely place. I have come to love the Lake Superior world more than any other and I can echo Yeats's poem about another, much smaller lake: "...always night and day/I hear lake water lapping with low sounds by the shore;/While I stand on the roadway, or on the pavement grey,/I hear it in the deep heart's core."

In those and other novels, I now see, my love for America had its origins. What I took from them was reinforced by some of the movies I knew in my youth, where I saw images of a land where even the destitute Okies had automobiles to travel to California in, a place of towering mountains and clear streams, cities of bursting energy, a country that yielded wealth to hard work. In movies, too, as well as in the comic books I was able to buy in Castleford market, I found American humor and comedy, different from ours, but engaging and fresh. And gradually I began to discern that the American notion of freedom was something that differed importantly from England's proscribed version. I, already a mildly rebellious subject of the King, was moving towards discovering a classless society, though that was not wholly clear to me until I was attached to the American army in Germany. I must admit, though, that, in my first weeks with my new colleagues, I had the same difficulty that the Germans had in dealing with the egalitarian ways of the Americans. (It isn't easy to break long habit.) The Germans called America "the land of boundless opportunity" and in Germany, working with Americans for two years, I came increasingly to understand the "bound" Europe to which America was being contrasted.

But my most direct and important access to America was through jazz. I had early become a fan of big swing bands, first the English ones I heard on the BBC: Joe Loss and Oscar Rabin. "The Melody Maker" (what a very English title that is for a journal that covered pop music and jazz!) taught me that they were pale imitations of American groups, but it wasn't until the American Armed Forces Network began its broadcasts in England that I had a regular opportunity to hear people like Benny Goodman, Artie Shaw, Tommy Dorsey, and the peerless Glen Miller band. Eventually I was able to afford to buy a few phonograph records and I wore out Glen Miller hits on a record player borrowed from Aunt Ethel.

Those masters of swing led me to Duke Ellington's great band and his complex music, and then to the small group jazz of Louis Armstrong, as well as to brilliant piano men. I graduated from Fats Waller and Albert Ammons to Art Tatum, whose touch and style I tried in vain to imitate. He remains for me the best of them all.

Jazz quickly became an object of serious interest to me and I read eagerly about its origins in New Orleans, its movement "up the river" to Chicago, and then its adoption by white musicians. I learned of George Gershwin's experiments in bringing jazz forms into orchestral treatments and I was able to persuade the master in charge of the morning music at CGS to play a part of the "Rhapsody in Blue" one morning. Encouraged by that, a couple of my Upper Sixth pals and I put forward the proposal that we be allowed to offer a week of jazz recordings in lieu of the classical pieces that were our usual fare.

Meeting resistance, we compromised on three mornings, with the master's stipulation that one of us would make a two-minute introduction each day, to explain to our schoolmates—and our teachers—what they were about to hear. Because we had but a few records between us to choose from, we had no great difficulty in deciding what we would play. I wrote the scripts for all three appearances, showing off my scholarly mastery, and Geoff Wardle began with Glen Miller's "In the Mood" to illustrate what swing was, as distinct from jazz. Our fellow pupils loved it, while our teachers looked suitably nauseated. The next day Ken Hammill followed with Duke Ellington's "I Got It Bad and That Ain't Good," this to show jazz idiom in big band treatment. Our schoolmates were a good deal less enthusiastic and the gym teacher got me aside to suggest that we consider dropping the third day, since his staff colleagues had been so perturbed by the "American noises" that came from the phonograph. But I had prepared to be clean-up hitter, with a text and a recording to illustrate the improvisational elements that were central to the jazz idiom. I wasn't going to be dissuaded. Swallowing my stage fright, I stood before the school and read my few lines of text, with an increasing sense that I should have been content to stop with "Rhapsody in Blue." My record was alto saxophonist Johnny Hodges, a personal hero, leading a small group in "Squatty Roo," lots of brilliant improvisation about a riff I can recall to this day. Alas, it went over like the proverbial lead balloon. Nobody hissed or booed, but I was eyed suspiciously by most of the school after that. The headmaster warned me again about the high risks of letting my hobbies distract me from what should be my consuming interests.

My pals and I, downcast by our failure to win converts, comforted ourselves with the bleak recognition that we had spent our school years among Philistines.

Chapter 14
A Nice Cup of Tea

I make it a point never to order hot tea in an American restaurant. I learned many years ago that the consequence would be my being brought a small teapot of hot water—or perhaps only a cup of hot water—and a tea bag. Now, I hasten to say that I have nothing against the tea bag; I use tea bags every day. No, the point is the temperature of the water. Yorkshire children are taught from the time they can understand the difference between hot and cold that tea must be made with *boiling* water. In my mother's family the rule was, "Always bring the teapot to the kettle, never the kettle to the pot." Tea will not mash properly, unless the water has boiled and, as that incantation suggests, the water mustn't be allowed to "get off the boil." A restaurant that boils the water, but then puts it into a cold tea pot and lets a waitress carry it the half-mile from the kitchen to my table, is out to ruin my day. So I have learned to say, "Thank you, I think I'll have decaf. Yes, with cream, please."

Let me go back to the tea bag for a moment. I consider it one of the happiest of American inventions, eliminating as it does all the messing

about with loose tea: measuring it out in spoonfuls, having to pour the tea through a strainer,
getting the sticky leaves out of the teapot. Ugh,
no loose tea for me! I can certainly hope that
the English, having discovered central heating a
few years ago, have now embraced the tea bag,
but I'm not optimistic. I think of my mother's
lip curling as she said, "Tea baaaag? Surely you
don't use tea bags, Bruce." I know that my
mother used to pray that I would be kept from
embracing all things American and I must
believe that her learning that I used tea bags
habitually was a final reason for her to wonder
about the efficacy of prayer.

There is one real problem with the tea bag. It
rules out loose tea leaves in the bottom of the
cup (unless, of course, you have carelessly torn
the bag when putting it in your teapot), and that
in turn rules out Aunt Sadie's telling your fortune. On the rare occasions when we were at
Uncle Tom's for tea, his wife would, with some
coy reluctance, agree to do "a reading." That
began with her swirling the last drops of tea
around in the cup of the fortune seeker and then
letting the tea settle. She would then carefully
drain off the liquid so as not to disturb the patterns of leaves that had settled into place. Then

she would ponder the shapes, her brow furrowed, lips pursed. "Hmm, a big bird... perhaps an aeroplane... a lot of trees... hmm, that looks like the front of a double decker bus...." Eventually she would claim to find a pattern among the several objects and would then venture a prediction about events in our life in the following week. For some reason she always insisted that the leaves revealed only things that were close at hand. Inevitably, a few days after a visit to Uncle Tom's my mother would say, "Do you remember what your Aunt Sadie said about the tea leaves in your Dad's cup? Well, I saw something in the paper this morning that made me think of that. She does seem to have a gift." I don't recall her predicting the Prince of Wales's getting involved with Mrs. Simpson (speaking of things American), or the Hindenburg disaster. Certainly not World War II. I think she stuck to smaller things in Allerton and Castleford.

For Yorkshire folk the drinking of tea is akin to the rites of a secular religion. They want it hot, strong, and often. There seems to be hardly an occasion in Yorkshire life when it is not appropriate to have a cup of tea. The first thing Aunt Ella did when she returned from a walk or a ride was to put the kettle on, even before she took off her coat, to make herself a nice cup of tea. Notice that a cup of tea is always called "nice." "Just let me pop the kettle on," a housewife will say to a visitor, "and we'll have a nice cup of tea." A break in routine is called a tea break, even if you prefer to have a Coke or a coffee. (Another thing to note: my kinfolk ask "Would you like a coffee?" just as they would ask "Would you like a glass of beer or a whiskey?"—making of coffee the occasional beverage that it is for most of them. You would almost never be asked, "Would you like tea?" because it is assumed that everybody would always like to have tea.)

"One for each person and one for the pot" is the litany that tells how many spoonfuls of loose tea leaves are required to make a pot of tea. That formula, I know from long experience, will produce tea so strong that you can stand the spoon up in it. Of course, that strength goes with the Yorkshire practice of putting a lot of sugar and milk in the cup. I am a drinker, an avid drinker, of weak tea. I use one tea bag for a pot that will give me three cups and I use neither sugar nor milk. So my parents' tea, as I unthinkingly drank it neat after my long absence from their home, was a shock to my system. My mother could never get used to the fact that I took neither sugar nor milk. As was her wont, she put milk into my cup when she did her own and my father's, unless I caught her hand in time. Her reason for doing that was that the tea would not then stain the cup. But when I reminded her that I didn't take milk, she would frown and say, "Well, you always did when you were at home." (That was her phrase for summing up all the evil ways I had fallen into in my army years and my exile in America.) I would remind her that I gave up sugar and milk early in the war, four years before I left for the army, recognizing the rationing we lived under. (My father gave up sugar, too, but he took it up again once rationing was over.) That did not silence my mother. She would dismiss my statement with a shake of her head and say, "Well, you are the only one in the family who does." I could never resist pointing out that Aunt Ella, her favorite sister, always drank tea neat, but that only elicited another rebuttal, "Well, Ella does have some peculiar tastes." A draw, until the next meal.

With the quantities of milk and sugar my parents put in their tea, the resulting drink was a hot tea sundae or something akin to that. My father always used three teaspoons of sugar in what was a relatively small cup, no pint pot of the kind I affected for a time, and both my parents used enough milk to turn the tea near white. The flavor of the tea remained, of course, with all those tea leaves they began with, but their idea of tea was so far removed from mine that we were nearly chalk and cheese.

My parents had tea at all four meals, almost never between meals. In that they were exceptional, for most Yorkshire people liked a mid-morning and a mid-afternoon cup of tea, as my grandparents did. My mother might pop the kettle on, if she had been out shopping or had just come in from the cold, but that was rare. In their tea-drinking habits they differed drastically from their closest friends, Harry and Cissie Mills. Those two were addicts, drinking tea at all hours of the day—and, believe it or not, in the middle of the night. After the war the Millses bought an electric kettle with a clock and timer that could be set to go off at three a.m., when they were awakened to water already on the boil. They had a nice cup of tea before going back to sleep. My mother told me of this as though she were revealing that Harry and Cissie had moved from marijuana to cocaine. I feigned shock and promised not to reveal their secret. They have been dead for many years, so I think it's OK for me now to talk about their addiction.

On one of my visits in the nineteen-seventies my mother cautiously told me that she had read in the paper that Americans had taken to drinking iced tea. "You don't do that, do you?" she asked me, looking a little anxious. I not only admitted that I did; I said I did it regularly and eagerly. "But how can you stand that for breakfast?" she asked, shock now registering. I explained that I drank only hot tea at breakfast and that iced tea was a refreshing summertime drink with lunch and even dinner. A wearied shake of the head: "Americans, Americans, they really are peculiar people." I could never convince her to give it a try.

I grew up drinking large quantities of tea and I still do. Everybody in my family was a heavy tea drinker and I thought for a long time that "tee-total" was spelled "tea-total," for we were totally committed to tea. My mother never allowed me to emulate my grandpa, who often poured his tea into his saucer to cool it and then slurped it down noisily. Neither did she allow me or my father to drink our tea out of anything but a china cup; it was a part of her civilizing process for us. Most of the men and boys in the village drank their tea out of a mug, a pint pot as it was usually called whether it actually held a pint or not. I, who liked labor saving in any form, thought a mug preferable to the constant passing back and forth of my cup for refills—I would often down five of those wee cups at a meal—and it did a better job of keeping the tea warm. On one extended visit to my parents I decided to buy myself a pint pot, but my mother's obvious pain caused me to pack it away in my bag for use when I should get back to America. My wife was equally displeased with that huge thing on the table and so it eventually found a place on my desk, a repository for pencils and ballpoint pens.

In my early years in Canada and America, particularly after my discovering what restaurants would pull on me if I asked for tea, I gave up on tea and drank coffee. I had discovered the pleasures of that beverage when I was working with Americans in Germany and my wife was a coffee drinker. It was easy to drink what others were drinking. By then the English were discovering coffee as an after-dinner drink and it has so grown in popularity that there are said to be Englishmen, though I think not Yorkshiremen, who prefer it to tea. Indeed, they have become self-proclaimed authorities on good coffee. I have read accounts of

travel in America written by English visitors to
this country, who are so convinced of the superi-
ority of England's coffee that they speak pityingly
of Americans who so rarely seem to get a decent
cup of coffee. They are the same English travelers,
I'm sure, who pity the French for the poor wine
they drink and the Germans for the awful beer
they have to put up with.

When I was sixteen and doubtless influenced
by my ever-growing interest in things American,
I decided to try coffee. The best I could do, in
that third year of the war, was to make myself a
cup of something called "Camp Coffee." That
had only indirect connection to coffee beans, I
must now think, but at the time I thought myself
very sophisticated to be trying it. It was made by
adding boiling water to a spoonful of a gooey
looking substance that contained chicory. That
was added for flavoring, it was said, though I now
wonder whether there was actually any coffee in
the concoction, so different from true coffee
does my memory recall the flavor of my new
drink. I remember it chiefly now for the bottle it
came in, square-sided and on the front a colored
picture, appropriate to the product's name, of a
kilted British officer sitting outside his tent, cup
at hand, and behind him a turbaned Indian ser-

vant. Both the image and the product survived long after the loss of Empire, certainly long enough for my daughter to bring a bottle back from England as a souvenir. She still has it, treasuring it as an emblem of political incorrectness and consumer fraud.

I never convinced my parents to try "Camp Coffee." I do remember my mother picking up the bottle from the table and looking critically at the label, even as I remember her saying, "I don't know why you get interested in things like this, Bruce."

Well, mother, you wanted me to be different.

Chapter 15
A Nice Place to Visit, But...

There is a poem of Heinrich Heine's that has always spoken to me in a special way. Living in exile for many years in Paris, he wrote of "dreaming of Germany in the night." I have my dreams. I dream of Yorkshire in the night, but not as Heine dreamed, not yearning for something denied me, not pining for a homeland that has spurned me. For I am no exile in a foreign country, as Heine was. I am where I wish to be, in a land that has taken me to its bosom and nurtured me. I am home. My recurring dreams are of childhood's place, where people speak to me in a tongue that was my "baby talk," a tongue I still understand but do not use. And sometimes in the day even, suddenly, taking me by surprise, my Yorkshire dialect rises up in me, amusing me and leaving me without any pain of remorse. I love it for its simple strength, its sometimes absurd phrasing, its monosyllabic words that can contain a whole sentence-worth of meaning. I hear Grandpa Street telling his buddy, Tommy Hutchinson, "A cud do wi' thee, Hutchy, butt tha's sa daft." ("I could put up with you, Hutchy, if you weren't so stupid.") Characteristically blunt, but with no real malice to it.

My favorite Yorkshire piece jumps up in my mind time and again. I once sent a note to Bill Bryson, the American travel writer, who lived in Yorkshire for several years, urging him to consider that the little poem I enclosed was more revealingly Yorkshire than "Ilkla Moor," which he had cited as his essential piece. I have no idea when I first learned these lines; they seem to have been part of me forever. I cherish them for their evoking the kind of exchange I have listened to a thousand times on Yorkshire streets and marketplaces. They have to be spoken with an air of wonderment that any such question could ever have been put to a man or that there is a world in which it might be important for one man—and a stranger at that—to understand whether another can dance. It is an exchange at the most rudimentary, monosyllabic level possible. It is, of course, a conversation that goes nowhere.

> A chap sez to me, "Can tha dance?"
> Ah sez, "Dance?" 'E sez, "Aye."
> Ah sez, "Who?" 'E sez, "Thee."
> Ah sez, "Me?" 'E sez, "Aye."
> Ah sez, "Aw."

That last "Aw" is the predictable end of many a Yorkshire discussion or argument. It signals "Very well, then" or "If that's your opinion, all right. I accept what you have told me." It is as indispensable to Yorkshire speech as "OK" is to American. It saves a lot of breath.

There is another indispensable monosyllable, heard as often as "Aw." It is "Eeeee." It can be used as a commentary, meaning "Is that so?" Used with an appropriate sinking inflection, it can be a sympathetic "How sad." With a rising inflection it can mean "That *is* a surprise." Or in its short form it can be simply a warm prelude to "Ahm reight glad ter see thee." You can't go very far in Yorkshire without it.

I love those monosyllables. I love every sound of the dialect; I cherish my memories of the childhood when it was my mother tongue. Yet it is not the great love of my life. Being American is.

I have embraced my American identity wholeheartedly and I never qualify my citizenship by saying, "Of course, in England we'd do it this way." When it is a matter of "You say tomahtoes, we say tomatoes," I am with the "we." My American habits are such that it takes a conscious effort when I am writing to an English cousin to write "serviette" for "napkin" or to use "Motorway" instead of "Interstate." In the fiftieth year of my citizenship I can think myself as American as those who were born here. My language is American, with a slight Yorkshire accent.

Yet I do not ever regret having been born and raised in Allerton Bywater. I have many a reason to be glad of the Yorkshire core to my being. I have often thought that I might not have found the study of language so absorbing, so central to my life, had I not so early begun to think on the differences between the sounds of my village's speech and the modulated tones of my schoolmasters. And I owe the ancient county of York much more than that.

But I have not gone back for visits since my mother died in 1986, twenty years now. I know why. In the time when I went back every summer, the decade between my father's death and my mother's, I found that three weeks was the absolute limit to my stay. Always at first, of course, there were the joys of seeing my mother and my kinfolk, of hearing the welcoming sounds of the dialect, and of retracing my childhood paths through the village. Yet the pleasures soon gave way to rising anger, as I encountered again the chilling omnipresence of monarchy and class system. I recognized again how much richer my parents' lives could have been in a society of citizens rather than subjects. I writhed as I watched my mother humble herself to shopkeepers and waiters she thought herself inferior to. Louder and louder as the days of my visits wore on, I heard the echoes of that childhood admonition, "Bruce, we have to know our place."

So now, with nearly all those good Yorkshire folk I loved gone to their Maker, I know that to visit would be only to see again why I had to leave. Better to stay away and let my Yorkshire live on in memory. And live it does.

Allerton Bywater will always be part of me, with its coal dust, its ugliness, and its rough, tough, enduring people. And with its woefully restricted life in that place of grinding work, work, work. But also with its warm fireplaces, hot tea and toast, gravy-soaked Yorkshire pudding, the laughter and joys of old friends. There is sometimes a voice I hear in the night that says, "Ah do luv thee."

About the Author

Bruce Haywood served as provost at Kenyon College in Ohio for seventeen years, and as president of Monmouth College in Illinois for fourteen years. Born in 1925 in York, England, he served with army intelligence in Germany at the end of World War II, then continued his education at Leeds University. He is a 1950 graduate of McGill University and earned a Harvard Ph.D. in 1956. His previous books include *The Essential College*, published by XOXOX Press in 2006. Bruce currently resides in Galesburg, Illinois.